A Road Beyond the Suffering

Kimberly,

Other than the Bible and The Baptist Hymnal, This book has helped me deal with my chronic Illnesses more than Anything Else.

I had the opportunity to set To Know the Authors during My OBU years. They Are Truely Remarkable in Both Their walk with The Lord & As Husband & wife.

I hope in These pages that you find A deeper understanding of The Lord, yourself, and how healthy people view us. Your wonderful Attitude and outlook on Life come Through online, But getting to meet you In person will be Truely special.

Thanks For The Memory :-) Love Todd

A Road Beyond the Suffering

An Experiential Journey through the Book of Job

Dick and Sue Rader

PROVIDENCE HOUSE PUBLISHERS
Franklin, Tennessee

Copyright 1997 by Dick and Sue Rader

Scripture taken from the *Holy Bible: New International Version®*. NIV®. Copyright © 1973, 1978, 1984 by International Bible Society. Used by permission of Zondervan Publishing House.

The "NIV" and "New International Version" trademarks are regis-tered in the United States Patent and Trademark Office by International Bible Society.

Printed in the United States of America

01   00   99   98   97   5   4   3   2   1

Library of Congress Catalog Card Number: 97-68561

ISBN: 1-57736-056-7

Cover by Bozeman Design; Background illustrations and concept by Sue Rader; Silhouette by Elaine Kernea

PROVIDENCE HOUSE PUBLISHERS
238 Seaboard Lane • Franklin, Tennessee 37067
800-321-5692

*"For everything
that was written in the past
was written to teach us,
so that through endurance
and the encouragement of the Scriptures
we might have hope."*

ROMANS 15:4

CONTENTS

Letters (cont.)

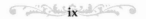

INTRODUCTION

The following is a series of letters that we wrote as a husband and wife who discovered the Book of Job in an intimate way in our marriage. During our second and third decades together, we were led through many of the experiences recounted by Job in the Bible. We experienced prolonged illness, loss of loved ones, loss of personal possessions, and loss of vocation.

Because of a debilitating physical ailment that struck in 1977 and refused to respond to treatment, Sue was unable to continue as a missionary in Zambia, a country in south central Africa where we had served since 1968. We were able to continue our missionary career temporarily by transferring to Johannesburg, South Africa, in early 1978, but in order to do so, we were forced to leave most of our worldly goods in Zambia. War for the independence of Zimbabwe, which was waging at that time, prevented overland shipment of our belongings. Only a limited number of books and keepsakes were shipped by air to our new home. We searched for meaning in all that was happening to us and found that God was sufficient for all of our needs.

After fourteen months of intense testing and experimentation with drugs, because of a lack of diagnosis Sue's doctors encouraged us to return to the United States. Again, we disposed of all our furniture and trimmed our books and memorabilia to a bare minimum. Since Sue was expected to receive proper medical treatment leading to a cure in the United States and our sending mission board anticipated our subsequent return to mission work, a full allowance for shipping our belongings at that time was not considered. During our year in South Africa, we also grieved because of the death of Sue's father.

Our return to our native land did not bring about the magical cure many had hoped for. Instead, we chased after medical solutions for an additional three years of tentative diagnoses and subsequent disappointments. At the end of that period, termination of what we had hoped would be a lifetime career in foreign mission work was inevitable. In April 1982, we submitted a letter of resignation to the Foreign Mission Board of the Southern Baptist Convention—now the International Mission Board.

Shortly after that fateful letter was sent, we experienced an unusual happening in the privacy of our home. On April 29, 1982, in a manner unexplainable other than by the grace of God, Sue was completely relieved of the pain that had increasingly tormented her day and night for almost five years.

For the next ten years, we were able to live a normal life and rebuild the physical structure of our home. Our five sons grew to manhood, and Dick became established as professor, then dean, and finally Vice President for Religious Life at Oklahoma Baptist University (OBU). Not wanting to separate ourselves completely from foreign missions, both of us became involved in the lives of missionary kids who had grown up in another culture and had chosen OBU for their college education. Dick's position enabled him to relate to foreign missionaries who had come to teach at OBU during their furloughs and gave him the opportunity to advise students who had felt God's call on their own lives. Again we suffered the grief of losing close loved ones in the deaths of Sue's mother and Dick's grandmother, who had greatly influenced his formative years.

In the early 1990s, Sue began to experience occasional backaches after prolonged heavy work. This seemed to be a normal part of aging for a woman recently past fifty, and so we saw no cause for worry. The yearly back spasm and swelling that inhibited reaching her feet for about a week was also explained away by recent sitting at the computer or reaching in an awkward position or merely lifting incorrectly.

In 1994, it became evident that the backaches were severely interfering with her daily activities and no longer to be ignored. The first doctor she saw attributed her pain to muscle weakness caused by an angiogram-related stroke during her earlier illness. The theory seemed feasible for about six months, but the increasing frequency and intensity of the back pain called for a second opinion. This examination resulted in further testing and referrals that finally led to a diagnosis in March of 1995 of extreme osteoporosis, such as is normally found only in women more than eighty years of age. Whether this had been brought about by any of the wide variety of medications during her earlier illness or was simply the normal result of a lifelong tendency toward thin bones is still in question. One fact was sure: Sue had always consumed sufficient quantities of calcium, which at some point her body had ceased to absorb.

Medications that were believed to have the capacity to stop the deterioration were tried and laid aside, either because they were ineffective or because of reactions that only increased the misery Sue was already experiencing. By late summer, Sue was relying heavily on a carefully planned diet, sufficient rest, as much exercise as possible without injury, and a welcome invention, the wheelchair (for trips outside her home). She lived as full a life as possible while she tried other medicines when they became available. She refused to give up and enjoyed frequent outings to church and campus events.

As physical problems continued to plague her, we grasped for every available means to find the intimacy we had lost somewhere in the maze of the past twenty years of pain and loss. God led us once more to the Book of Job and to another who struggled with difficult questions. One day in late spring of 1995, Sue was impressed that reading aloud might lend new meaning to these passages. She found that the entire Book of Job can be read aloud in about three hours. From Sue relating how meaningful this experience had been for her, Dick was encouraged to begin reading the book once more himself. That evening he had some comments on the opening chapters. In our thirty-fifth year as husband and wife, we decided to write down the thoughts we wanted to share with each other about Job.

Soon those letters were becoming this book. Since our primary focus was on the message of Job, we attempted to include all of the verses found in that writing. The quotations of Scripture in our letters come from the New International Version of the Bible (Zondervan 1984). We italicized words in Scripture that we wanted to emphasize to each other. Our outline will help in finding questions that are vexing our readers. At the end of the book, we have included several charts that enabled us to see more clearly some of the relationships we found in our reading. We also prepared a sequential index so that if our readers wished to find our comments on a particular passage, they would be able to do so.

Like us, do you struggle to reconcile a strong belief in God's goodness, justice, and unsurpassed power with personal life-changing experiences? Are you tired of trite answers that bring no comfort to your troubled soul? We open our personally disturbing questions and some of the answers we found in Job to you, our readers. As God revealed Himself in ways we had not seen before, we began to discover the comfort hidden there. As you follow our winding trail of thoughts in search of the truth that God wants to reveal to all people, our prayer is not that you would find our answers but that you would be able to hear God answering your own questions in a personal way that applies precisely to your pain and that you will discover the comfort your soul craves.

A Road
Beyond the
Suffering

LETTERS

How Can God Love Me and
Still Let Me Suffer So Much?

Dearest Dick,

When you came home at noon you discovered me reading the Book of Job. I silently finished it within the next minute or two. Since 9:00 I had wept my way through reading aloud the entire story of Job. I found passages I don't remember ever seeing before. This one really caught my attention.

> "The dead are in deep anguish, those beneath the waters and all that live in them. Death is naked before God; Destruction lies uncovered. He spreads out the northern skies over empty space; he suspends the earth over nothing. He wraps up the waters in his clouds, yet the clouds do not burst under their weight. He covers the face of the full moon, spreading his clouds over it. He marks out the horizon on the face of the waters for a boundary between light and darkness. The pillars of the heavens quake, aghast at his rebuke. By his power he churned up the sea; by his wisdom he cut Rahab to pieces. By his breath the skies became fair; his hand pierced the gliding serpent. And these are but the outer fringe of his works; how faint the whisper we hear of him! Who then can understand the thunder of his power?" (26:5–14)

Other books in the Bible include some of these ideas, but I don't think I have ever heard them so exquisitely expressed. Perhaps I don't know as much about God as I thought. How can God love me and still let me suffer so much?

I love you,
Sue

Why Should I Struggle in Vain?

Dearest Darling,

Although I have yet to read all of Job, and I did not read it aloud, I too have found some marvelous "gems" that speak to me. Some of it is perplexing,

1

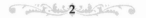

especially when we try to apply it to our situation. At times Job seemed to say one thing and then almost contradict it later.

In 7:17–21 he speaks of the wonder and yet perplexity of God's constant care for us.

> "What is man that you make so much of him, that you give him so much attention, that you examine him every morning and test him every moment? Will you never look away from me, or let me alone even for an instant? If I have sinned, what have I done to you, O watcher of men? Why have you made me your target? Have I become a burden to you? Why do you not pardon my offenses and forgive my sins? For I will soon lie down in the dust; you will search for me, but I will be no more."

This struck my attention because I sometimes marvel that God knows and cares so much for me. Unlike Job at this point, I am so thankful that God does forgive me—over and over again. You have done that too! I am so thankful that you love me so much and that you forgive me when I stumble in our relationship.

The other passage I discovered is 9:27–28.

> "If I say, 'I will forget my complaint, I will change my expression, and smile,' I still dread all my sufferings, for I know you will not hold me innocent."

However, I'm not sure I understand verses 29–31.

> "Since I am already found guilty, why should I struggle in vain? Even if I washed myself with soap and my hands with washing soda, you would plunge me into a slime pit so that even my clothes would detest me."

I love you,
Dick

LETTER 3

God Is Wooing Me from
the Jaws of Distress

Dearest Dick,

I have sometimes felt like verses 29–31. They *are* hard to understand. I think it is because Job had not yet learned the truth in 1:1–2:8. If only he had known:

The Lord said to Satan, "Very well, then, everything he has is in your hands, but on the man himself do not lay a finger." (1:12a)

The Lord said to Satan, "Very well, then, he is in *your* hands; but you must spare his life." (2:6)

If only we could always remember that God never wills us evil but is always working to redeem us as he says through his messenger in 36:15–16:

"But those who suffer he delivers in their suffering; he speaks to them in their affliction.

"He is wooing you from the jaws of distress. . . ."

I have sometimes been like Job in our relationship and blamed you, the one who loves me, for my pain. Forgive me. I didn't understand how much you wanted to deliver me from my suffering but just didn't know how.

Love,
Sue

LETTER 4

My Intercessor Pleads with God on My Behalf

Dearest Sue,

Thank you for the insight from chapters 1 and 2. I had not thought of that. It is so important for us to remember that God really does love us—no matter what—and he wants the best for us. I have found that it also helps me in our relationship to remember that you really do love me—no matter what. I love you that way too.

Today I found another "gem" from Job. In the midst of his intense suffering when he actually seemed to blame God for his calamity, he gave a mighty cry of faith.

"O earth, do not cover my blood; may my cry never be laid to rest! Even now *my witness* is in heaven; *my advocate* is on high. *My intercessor* is *my friend* as my eyes

pour out tears to God; on behalf of a man he pleads with God as a man pleads for his friend." (16:18–21)

It seems that Job had insight into the coming "comforter," the Holy Spirit Jesus promised in John 14.

I love you,
Dick

LETTER 5

The Fear of the Lord Is Wisdom

Dearest Dick,

The Holy Spirit is not the only New Testament concept in Job. Here is the most unusual passage on salvation I have found in the Bible. What a picture of "falling short of the glory of God!" The Lord challenged Job:

> "Would you discredit my justice? Would you condemn me to justify yourself? Do you have an arm like God's, and can your voice thunder like his? Then adorn yourself with glory and splendor, and clothe yourself in honor and majesty. Unleash the fury of your wrath, look at every proud man and bring him low, look at every proud man and humble him, crush the wicked where they stand. Bury them all in the dust together; shroud their faces in the grave. Then I myself will admit to you that your own right hand can save you." (40:8–14)

We can't save ourselves. God alone is standing against all the wickedness of the world just for us. Isn't that wonderful? In no way could we do this. What fools we are when we fall into Satan's trap of self-deception and try.

No wonder God Himself says the "fear of the Lord" is wisdom. I had always thought that phrase came from James or Proverbs or Ecclesiastes. But just look at chapter 28. God Himself said it!

> "There is a mine for silver and a place where gold is refined. Iron is taken from the earth, and copper is smelted from ore. Man puts an end to the darkness; he searches the farthest recesses for ore in the blackest darkness. Far from where people dwell he cuts a shaft, in places forgotten by the foot of man; far from men he dangles and sways. The earth, from which food comes, is transformed below

as by fire; sapphires come from its rocks, and its dust contains nuggets of gold. No bird of prey knows that hidden path, no falcon's eye has seen it. Proud beasts do not set foot on it, and no lion prowls there. Man's hand assaults the flinty rock and lays bare the roots of the mountains. He tunnels through the rock; his eyes see all its treasures. He searches the sources of the rivers and brings hidden things to light.

"But where can wisdom be found? Where does understanding dwell? Man does not comprehend its worth; it cannot be found in the land of the living. The deep says, 'It is not in me'; the sea says, 'It is not with me.' It cannot be bought with the finest gold, nor can its price be weighed in silver. It cannot be bought with the gold of Ophir, with precious onyx or sapphires. Neither gold nor crystal can compare with it, nor can it be had for jewels of gold. Coral and jasper are not worthy of mention; the price of wisdom is beyond rubies. The topaz of Cush cannot compare with it; it cannot be bought with pure gold.

"Where then does wisdom come from? Where does understanding dwell? It is hidden from the eyes of every living thing, concealed even from the birds of the air. Destruction and Death say, 'Only a rumor of it has reached our ears.' God understands the way to it and he alone knows where it dwells, for he views the ends of the earth and sees everything under the heavens. When he established the force of the wind and measured out the waters, when he made a decree for the rain and a path for the thunderstorm, then he looked at wisdom and appraised it; he confirmed it and tested it. And he said to man, 'The fear of the Lord—that is wisdom, and to shun evil is understanding.'" (28:1–28)

I've always felt that I made so many mistakes as a parent: I wasn't at the right place at the right time. I didn't prepare them for every situation. I couldn't teach them everything I knew. I couldn't help them do all of the things I never learned myself but wished I had. I sometimes embarrassed them with my thoughtless comments. I couldn't rubber-stamp all of my values on their hearts. I couldn't stand between them and heartache. I couldn't communicate to them how completely and unreservedly I loved every one of them. I couldn't convince them how proud I was of the uniqueness of each one. I passed on to them some of my own inadequacies. After studying these passages from Job, I now realize that if my children believe that the fear of the Lord is wisdom and to shun evil is understanding, and they learned that from me, I don't have to worry about the mistakes anymore.

I love you,
Sue

6

LETTER 6

Wise Men Do Not Give Traditional Answers

Darling Sue,

Truly we are powerless to save ourselves, and it is an awesome thought to realize that in our helplessness our God stands to save us. I believe God has enabled us to give our children a strong sense of the "fear of the Lord." I pray they will always reverence Him, regardless of their circumstances.

One who truly "fears the Lord" does not have all the answers. Job's frustration with his friends was that they espoused simple, traditional answers.

> "But come on, all of you, try again! I will not find a wise man among you. My days have passed, my plans are shattered, and so are the desires of my heart. These men turn night into day; in the face of darkness they say, 'Light is near.' If the only home I hope for is the grave, if I spread out my bed in darkness, if I say to corruption, 'You are my father,' and to the worm, 'My mother' or 'My sister,' where then is my hope? Who can see any hope for me? Will it go down to the gates of death? Will we descend together into the dust?" (17:10–16)

Many times over the past years some of our friends have been like Job's. They have hurt you deeply by giving "pat" answers. I fear that I too may have been superficial in some of my responses to your questions. I now see that having the "fear of the Lord" is the wisdom that counts. In our "fear" we trust Him, His ability, and His desire to give us the best!

I love you,
Dick

LETTER 7

I Just Want to Be Me,
but My Body Won't Let Me

Dearest Dick,

It's true! Some of the deepest hurts of my life have come through the words of my friends who thought they were being helpful. One of the most flippant comforts I have received over and over reminds me of the one from chapter 9, which you mentioned the other day. It comes in many forms: "Surely it's

not that bad. Smile! Things will get better" or "You can't? Oh, but you will" or "The doctors will be able to help you. They just haven't figured out how to yet, or God just hasn't shown them how to yet."

What a disservice to everyone are those who say that people who follow God find Him just like they themselves wish Him to be. What a denial of who He really is! For instance, this passage:

> "Blessed is the man whom God corrects; so do not despise the discipline of the Almighty. For he wounds, but he also binds up; he injures, but his hands also heal. From six calamities he will rescue you; in seven no harm will befall you. In famine he will ransom you from death, and in battle from the stroke of the sword. You will be protected from the lash of the tongue, and need not fear when destruction comes. You will laugh at destruction and famine, and need not fear the beasts of the earth. For you will have a covenant with the stones of the field, and the wild animals will be at peace with you. You will know that your tent is secure; you will take stock of your property and find nothing missing. You will know that your children will be many, and your descendants like the grass of the earth. You will come to the grave in full vigor, like sheaves gathered in season.

> "We have examined this, and it is true." (5:17–27a)

What about those African Christians who have died along with others in recent famine or those Christians in many countries who have succumbed to the AIDS epidemic? How does this comfort the family of the Christian soldier who has died in battle? Job was suffering at that very moment from Eliphaz's tongue because he was denying everything that had happened to Job. We instinctively stay clear of the bear and the lion because we know their appetite is not selective for the Christian or the nonchristian. What a cruel statement for the childless to hear! Would he deny the commitment of all those dear saints who have died a painful death due to disease or war?

How do I explain to a world who has not experienced "the ultimate grief: losing one's self" that I am just trying to find the guts to go on? I just want to be the same person I always was, but my body won't let me. How can they know how much I want them to be right, but in my heart I know they are dead wrong!

Thank you, God, for the Book of Job! You expose the lies for what they are. The truths therein are my comfort!

Love,
Sue

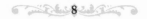

Job Felt Alone Because He Felt
Wronged by God

Dearest Darling,

Being alone is terrible! I know that you have felt alone often when no one understood. We have both felt alone when our relationship was strained. When I am unable to talk with you, I feel so alone and do not even want to talk with God.

It is hard to imagine how alone Job felt, even in the midst of friends. Job felt wronged by God. He still wanted to talk with God, but seemingly he couldn't.

> "Though I cry, 'I've been wronged!' I get no response; though I call for help, there is no justice. He has blocked my way so I cannot pass; he has shrouded my paths in darkness. He has stripped me of my honor and removed the crown from my head. He tears me down on every side till I am gone; he uproots my hope like a tree." (19:7–10)

What intrigues me about this speech by Job is that in the midst of his loneliness and hopelessness, he still could look to God as his Redeemer with confidence. He wanted everyone to know that he believed he would see God one day and that made all the difference.

> "Oh, that my words were recorded, that they were written on a scroll, that they were inscribed with an iron tool on lead, or engraved in rock forever! I know that my Redeemer lives, and that in the end he will stand upon the earth. And after my skin has been destroyed, yet in my flesh I will see God; I myself will see him with my own eyes—I, and not another. How my heart yearns within me!" (19:23–27)

I hope neither of us feels alone again. Hopefully I can be more understanding of you and your feelings so you will know that I am truly walking with you. I also want our communication to improve to the point that we will always be able to talk with each other, regardless of the circumstances. However, whether or not we ever do feel alone again, I hope we can have Job's faith. He kept on believing God—even through his frustrations!

I love you,
Dick

Words Cannot Comfort When I Cannot Pray

Dearest Dick,

It's so hard to know what to say to someone who is hurting even if it's your spouse. I was talking recently with a friend who is struggling with this problem. She is acquainted with families who are being touched by AIDS. What do you say? "I know how you feel"? Wrong. Wrong. Wrong.

My friend and I concluded that "I hurt because you hurt" may be all we *can* say truthfully. Trying to help figure out the whys is surely the broad road to inflicting more pain. I know that from experience.

The most comforting thing Job's three friends did may have been recorded in 2:11–13:

> When Job's three friends, Eliphaz the Temanite, Bildad the Shuhite and Zophar the Naamathite, heard about all the troubles that had come upon him, they set out from their homes and met together by agreement to go and sympathize with him and comfort him. When they saw him from a distance, they could hardly recognize him; they began to weep aloud, and they tore their robes and sprinkled dust on their heads. Then they sat on the ground with him for seven days and seven nights. No one said a word to him, because they saw how great his suffering was.

Maybe Job was just asking for it when he himself broke the silence. He did not doubt the sympathy he saw in his friends' demeanor and their inability to speak. But maybe he thought they could sympathize even more if they could understand just how deep his anguish was in his own eyes.

The first words out of Eliphaz's mouth were spoken with caution.

> "If someone ventures a word with you, will you be impatient? But who can keep from speaking?" (4:2)

But his words were still hurtful. For example, Eliphaz said:

> "Think how you have instructed many, how you have strengthened feeble hands. Your words have supported those who stumbled; you have strengthened faltering knees. But now trouble comes to you, and you are discouraged; it strikes

you, and you are dismayed. Should not your piety be your confidence and your blameless ways your hope?" (4:3–6)

Part of Job's pain was already that he no longer could encourage others and his former words of encouragement suddenly tasted like a lie. He even questioned whether the others he had tried to encourage had felt that his words were shallow and that he didn't understand just as he was now perceiving his friends. I have received my friends words with that same uncertainty.

In spite of Job's discomfort, Eliphaz went on and on with his advice. He elaborated on how completely God destroys the wicked by comparing their plight to the lion with broken teeth (4:9–11). Unaware that Satan sometimes masquerades as a guiding spirit, Eliphaz even encouraged Job to rely on the message he brought because of its source:

"A word was secretly brought to me, my ears caught a whisper of it. Amid disquieting dreams in the night, when deep sleep falls on men, fear and trembling seized me and made all my bones shake. A spirit glided past my face, and the hair on my body stood on end. It stopped, but I could not tell what it was. A form stood before my eyes, and I heard a hushed voice: 'Can a mortal be more righteous than God? Can a man be more pure than his Maker? If God places no trust in his servants, if he charges his angels with error, how much more those who live in houses of clay, whose foundations are in the dust, who are crushed more readily than a moth! Between dawn and dusk they are broken to pieces; unnoticed, they perish forever. Are not the cords of their tent pulled up, so that they die without wisdom?'" (4:12–21)

Just as Satan took a truth and twisted it into a lie to deceive Eve in Genesis 3, he began here with a statement that sounded like the truth. He cleverly used it to deceive Eliphaz, who believed the lie and then passed it on to Job as the truth (compare to 9:2).

Using this lie as a springboard, Eliphaz then went on in 5:1–7 to prove its "truth" by his own observations until he got to 5:8 and said:

"But if it were I, I would. . . ."

In this case, Eliphaz recommended that Job appeal to God. He didn't understand that the greatest source of Job's pain was that he *could not* pray. What anguish of soul one goes through in the realization that the tried truisms do not apply! And how that pain multiplies when a friend says:

"So hear it and apply it to yourself." (5:27b)

Love,
Sue

*I Would Choose Praising God
Over Questioning*

Darling Sue,

I guess we all at some time would like for life to fall into a neat, predictable pattern. We see this, I think, in society's effort to make everyone "normal" or at least like some other segment of society.

Job's friends thought life did fit into a neat design, but Job knew differently. For example, he knew that not all wicked people suffer calamity—some live to a ripe old age. He questioned:

> "Why do the wicked live on, growing old and increasing in power? They see their children established around them, their offspring before their eyes. Their homes are safe and free from fear; the rod of God is not upon them. Their bulls never fail to breed; their cows calve and do not miscarry. They send forth their children as a flock; their little ones dance about. They sing to the music of tambourine and harp; they make merry to the sound of the flute. They spend their years in prosperity and go down to the grave in peace. Yet they say to God, 'Leave us alone! We have no desire to know your ways. Who is the Almighty, that we should serve him? What would we gain by praying to him?' But their prosperity is not in their own hands, so I stand aloof from the counsel of the wicked." (21:7–16)

There have been times when I have looked jealously at wealthy, wicked people. I have sometimes questioned why we did not have more, especially when the demands of our growing family were ever increasing. I have not understood why some things have happened to us and why some other people seem to get along fine and seemingly have no hardship. And I still don't have answers for all of these questions.

> "Can anyone teach knowledge to God, since he judges even the highest?"(21:22)

I have come to realize that God has cared for us and He continues to care for us. We really have never been destitute, and we have so much for which to be thankful. Our children are well and prospering. They love us, and they all are godly men and good husbands.

It is more fun to praise and thank God than to spend time trying to figure out answers to questions that really are not important.

I love you!
Dick

 **LETTER 11**

Pain Dims My View and
Questions Become Inevitable

Dearest Dick,

Praising God *is* more fun than pondering perplexing questions, but when I am bewildered by pain, fun becomes impossible and questions inevitable. I have wanted to say to some of my well-meaning friends just what Job said:

> "Doubtless you are the people, and wisdom will die with you! But I have a mind as well as you; I am not inferior to you. Who does not know all these things?" (12:2–3)

In trying to comfort me, so many people tell me things that I already know that I begin to believe they must think that I don't have a mind of my own. Life is such a puzzle, sometimes I begin to think maybe they're right. But I long to hold on to my integrity just as much as Job did.

> "Teach me, and I will be quiet; show me where I have been wrong. How painful are honest words! But what do your arguments prove? Do you mean to correct what I say, and treat the words of a despairing man as wind? You would even cast lots for the fatherless and barter away your friend.

> "But now be so kind as to look at me. Would I lie to your face? Relent, do not be unjust; reconsider, for my integrity is at stake. Is there any wickedness on my lips? Can my mouth not discern malice?" (6:24–30)

> "As surely as God lives, who has denied me justice, the Almighty, who has made me taste bitterness of soul, as long as I have life within me, the breath of God in my nostrils, my lips will not speak wickedness, and my tongue will utter no deceit. I will never admit you are in the right; till I die, I will not deny my integrity. I will maintain my righteousness and never let go of it; my conscience will not reproach me as long as I live." (27:2–6)

Job knew that he had regularly brought not only his own sins but the sins of his children before God (1:5). And he had trusted God for forgiveness. He honestly knew that he had faith in God and that he was clean because God had forgiven him. Yet his body was so distorted by pain his friends could not even look at him. All they could say was, "You must have done something really wicked. Confess!" or "If you just had more faith, everything would be all right." Those words surely do sound familiar! How painful it is to know that I am clean because God has been faithful to His promise and forgiven me and that my faith in Him is strong—but to hear a friend suggest that it is not so.

I have often wished for Job's courage in 13:1–12:

> "My eyes have seen all this, my ears have heard and understood it. What you know, I also know; I am not inferior to you. But I desire to speak to the Almighty and to argue my case with God. You, however, smear me with lies; you are worthless physicians, all of you! If only you would be altogether silent! For you, that would be wisdom. Hear now my argument; listen to the plea of my lips. Will you speak wickedly on God's behalf? Will you speak deceitfully for him? Will you show him partiality? Will you argue the case for God? Would it turn out well if he examined you? Could you deceive him as you might deceive men? He would surely rebuke you if you secretly showed partiality. Would not his splendor terrify you? Would not the dread of him fall on you? Your maxims are proverbs of ashes; your defenses are defenses of clay."

Those *proverbs of ashes* are but sweet, hollow assurances. They have already been burned up in the crucible of pain. Nothing remains but a shell that sounds sweet to the ears but turns bitter in the heart. The truth has long ceased to dwell in those empty words.

Job knew in his heart that God was his only hope. That is why he said:

> "Keep silent and let me speak; then let come to me what may. Why do I put myself in jeopardy and take my life in my hands? Though he slay me, yet will I hope in him; I will surely defend my ways to his face. Indeed, this will turn out for my deliverance, for no godless man would dare come before him!" (13:13–16)

It was because in his heart he believed that God is righteous and just, that he continued in verses 17–28:

> "Listen carefully to my words; let your ears take in what I say. Now that I have prepared my case, I know I will be vindicated. Can anyone bring charges against me? If so, I will be silent and die.
>
> "Only grant me these two things, O God, and then I will not hide from you: Withdraw your hand far from me, and stop frightening me with your terrors. Then summon me and I will answer, or let me speak, and you reply. How many

wrongs and sins have I committed? Show me my offense and my sin. Why do you hide your face and consider me your enemy? Will you torment a windblown leaf? Will you chase after dry chaff? For you write down bitter things against me and make me inherit the sins of my youth. You fasten my feet in shackles; you keep close watch on all my paths by putting marks on the soles of my feet.

"So man wastes away like something rotten, like a garment eaten by moths."

Job wondered why God was punishing him so, but he still trusted God to know what He was doing.

In the opening verses of chapter 14, he described man before God as the sages of his time had explained this relationship.

"Man born of woman is of few days and full of trouble. He springs up like a flower and withers away; like a fleeting shadow, he does not endure. Do you fix your eye on such a one? Will you bring him before you for judgment? Who can bring what is pure from the impure? No one! Man's days are determined; you have decreed the number of his months and have set limits he cannot exceed. So look away from him and let him alone, till he has put in his time like a hired man.

"At least there is hope for a tree: If it is cut down, it will sprout again, and its new shoots will not fail. Its roots may grow old in the ground and its stump die in the soil, yet at the scent of water it will bud and put forth shoots like a plant. But man dies and is laid low; he breathes his last and is no more. As water disappears from the sea or a riverbed becomes parched and dry, so man lies down and does not rise; till the heavens are no more, men will not awake or be roused from their sleep." (14:1–12)

But in verses 13–17, he begged God for hope of deliverance. He had no way of knowing that Jesus would say, "I am the resurrection. . . ."

"If only you would hide me in the grave and conceal me till your anger has passed! If only you would set me a time and then remember me! If a man dies, will he live again? All the days of my hard service I will wait for my renewal to come. You will call and I will answer you; you will long for the creature your hands have made. Surely then you will count my steps but not keep track of my sin. My offenses will be sealed up in a bag; you will cover over my sin." (14:13–17)

And in verses 18-22, he described the depth of anguish he felt because he had not seen the assurance of that deliverance:

"But as a mountain erodes and crumbles and as a rock is moved from its place, as water wears away stones and torrents wash away the soil, so you destroy man's hope. You overpower him once for all, and he is gone; you change his countenance and send him away. If his sons are honored, he does not know it; if they are brought low, he does not see it. He feels but the pain of his own body and mourns only for himself." (14:18–22)

We are more fortunate than Job because the Messiah has come and we know He will deliver us. We have experienced His presence many times. He has delivered us from poverty, from pain, from hopelessness in the past. Yet pain still has that power to dim our view. If only those who have never walked in our shoes could believe that pain can do that, perhaps there would not be so many sweet, hollow assurances.

I love you,
Sue

LETTER 12

Does Letting Us Suffer
Bring Glory to God?

Dear Sue,

Another attitude in the speech of Eliphaz and prevalent today is that God really doesn't care about the details of our lives. Notice his initial question.

"Can a man be of benefit to God? Can even a wise man benefit him? What pleasure would it give the Almighty if you were righteous? What would he gain if your ways were blameless?" (22:2–3)

I cannot agree with the point that Eliphaz seems to be making. I believe it does give God pleasure when we are righteous and it grieves Him when we are unrighteous. Don't we "glorify" Him by our acts of goodness? Jesus said we should do good works and so glorify our Heavenly Father (Matthew 5:16). Doesn't that benefit God and His Kingdom? If our ways are blameless, He should be glorified.

Having said this about our relationship with God, this does cause me to question whether or not God is concerned about our suffering. Sometimes it seems that God just lets us suffer, perhaps even for long periods of time. Does that bring glory to God?

I guess the answer is that our suffering *can* bring glory to Him. The New Testament tells us that these "trials" can strengthen us and mature our faith (James 1:2–4; 1 Peter 1:6–7). We're told that God's power is made manifest in our weakness (2 Corinthians 12:9).

As I think about Job, I see him bend as the winds of adversity and pain swept over him, but he never broke. He defied his friends' "counsel and the wisdom of the ages." He insisted that his calamity was not a result of sin and there must be some other explanation. He continued to plead with God for an audience with the Almighty.

I admire him! He is a good example to follow. I'm glad he persisted and did not give in to his friends. And you know what? I'm glad you are so strong and that you stand firm in your faith.

I love you *so* much!
Dick

LETTER 13

Feeling Forsaken by God, We Long for Days When He Seemed Near

Dearest Dick,

Sometimes I *am* strong. I know that at those times I have God to thank for the strength. When, in 1978, we had to leave everything behind in Zambia—all our furniture from our first seventeen years together and most of our wedding mementos—and then again when a year later we left even more belongings behind in South Africa, I think I could have echoed Job's words in 1:20–22.

> At this, Job got up and tore his robe and shaved his head. Then he fell to the ground in worship and said:
>
> "Naked I came from my mother's womb, and naked I will depart. The Lord gave and the Lord has taken away; may the name of the Lord be praised."

In all this, Job did not sin by charging God with wrongdoing.

God also gave me the perspective to say, "We lost only things. All that is really valuable we still have."

It was harder in South Africa because we had to ask the boys to leave behind all their Christmas gifts and it was only February. Our move would require them to abandon friendships they had spent months to make. I remember telling the boys to recall how God had been faithful in our transfer from Zambia to South Africa. We assured them that God would be just as faithful in our leaving South Africa for America. I needed that assurance as much as they did.

When I was sick in Zambia for five months and then for the entire year in South Africa, I did not feel forsaken. Even during the three years that followed in the United States, my faith hardly wavered. I do remember a few times when the pain was so bad I just couldn't form the words to pray. But I could feel the Spirit groaning for me at those times.

I was so glad when my healing in 1982 could bring glory to God. I was actually grateful that God had waited to heal me until my friends really believed I was sick, that faking such an illness was impossible. Even today when God prepares someone to hear about my healing, I try in telling the story to give Him all the glory.

I learned so much about God during those years of sickness. And you learned so much as you walked through them by my side. We could never have learned those lessons from men. Somehow these topics never came up in Sunday school or were preached from any pulpit. We both said that "the price was not too great to pay."

We even said that we "would go through it all again" to learn those lessons. How presumptuous! Just because we have strength to stand through a trial once doesn't guarantee the next time. Look at how many have fallen to repeated temptations because they proudly withstood the first.

This present illness has been harder. There have been victories for sure—like my asking the church to pray that I would have the strength to make the visit to Africa in April 1994. I was completely pain free from the time I stepped on the plane in Oklahoma City until we were home again. But, oh, the pain the next day!

I guess the hardest part of it all has been the sense of losing myself. This has been magnified by the fact that others also sometimes think of me as if I were a thing of the past. For instance, a man who was recently complimenting my singing said, "I'll bet you *used to be* a singer."

If I had not wanted to spare his feelings, I might have replied, "I still am." Instead, I died a little inside. I think I know exactly how Job felt when he said:

> "How I long for the months gone by, for the days when God watched over me, when his lamp shone upon my head and by his light I walked through darkness! Oh, for the days when I was in my prime, when God's intimate friendship blessed my house, when the Almighty was still with me and my children were around me, when my path was drenched with cream and the rock poured out for me streams of olive oil." (29:2–6)

I too long for days gone by. For instance, I find it extremely difficult to converse with anyone face to face like before. For some unexplainable reason (perhaps their mothers told them never to stand in front of anything with wheels) my friends move to the side of my wheelchair to talk to me. As the crick in my neck develops, I gently ease my chair around to face them, and they immediately maneuver to my side once more. The problem is particularly vexing at gatherings where I encounter a number of old acquaintances. I can't even relate to my children like I used to. Sometimes my pain has become a barrier between us. They have felt like they must walk on eggshells around me lest they add to my pain, or they have thought that they should give me advice to try to help me overcome the suffering. Both have only intensified the hurt. Nevertheless, I am still their mother, and I am in the present tense. But no matter how well my family can adjust, I have felt so weak—so forsaken—so shut out by God. How can anyone empathize with my desperation?

Love,
Sue

*When We Think We Have Nothing
to Hang Onto, God Cares*

Dearest Sue,

I know that I really can't relate to the intensity of your hurt or your loneliness. I try to feel with you, but I know that what you are experiencing is beyond my own comprehension because I have not had that kind of pain. Nevertheless, I hope that you know how much I suffer with you. Because you hurt, I hurt. When you feel alone, I hurt with you. When people don't know how to relate to you, I feel something of your frustration.

This seems to be what Job felt. He just wanted his friends to understand how he felt. Their responses to him were totally inappropriate even though they were the acceptable answers of the day.

Because of his illness, Job also felt distanced from God as reflected in his reply to Eliphaz.

> "Even today my complaint is bitter; his hand is heavy in spite of my groaning. If only I knew where to find him; if only I could go to his dwelling! I would state my case before him and fill my mouth with arguments. I would find out what he would answer me, and consider what he would say. Would he oppose me with great power? No, he would not press charges against me. There an upright man could present his case before him, and I would be delivered forever from my judge.
>
> "But if I go to the east, he is not there; if I go to the west, I do not find him. When he is at work in the north, I do not see him; when he turns to the south, I catch no glimpse of him." (23:2–9)

He had felt so close to God throughout his life. He was faithful in following God's way.

> "But he knows the way that I take; when he has tested me, I will come forth as gold. My feet have closely followed his steps; I have kept to his way without turning aside. I have not departed from the commands of his lips; I have treasured the words of his mouth more than my daily bread." (23:10–12)

He too was very frustrated! Where was the reward for following God's way that we so often talk about? Where was the "It Pays to Serve Jesus"? Job felt like he couldn't even find God to talk with him.

It's interesting the way Job spoke of his "fear of the Lord."

> "But he stands alone, and who can oppose him? He does whatever he pleases. He carries out his decree against me, and many such plans he still has in store. That is why I am terrified before him; when I think of all this, I fear him. God has made my heart faint; the Almighty has terrified me. Yet I am not silenced by the darkness, by the thick darkness that covers my face." (23:13–17)

He seems to shrug his shoulders and say, "Oh, well, God is God and He will do what He wants to, and there is nothing we can do about it." Is that the way it is?

No, I really believe God cares about us, even though there are times when it doesn't look that way. There were times during your earlier illness when everything looked very dark. Those frustrating visits to doctors when we were told they did not know what was wrong with you were difficult times. However, we learned much and grew in our relationship with God during those days. He taught us about His sufficiency in every situation. From this we learned about the relationship between His faithfulness and our faith in Him. God taught us more about life than we could ever have imagined!

I hope the same is true now. I don't know what all God wants to teach us, but I hope we can be teachable. I feel that I am gaining a new respect or "fear" of God from this study of Job's experience. But I still hold to the truth that was so evident from our earlier experience. God loves us and wants the best for us.

I love you,
Dick

LETTER 15

God's Purpose Is So Much Wider
Than We Imagine

Dearest Dick,

Without really looking at chapters 1 and 2, I think Job is a book about hopelessness. But when I study the opening verses very closely I find the hope that sustained Job even when he stood apart from his friends.

> In the land of Uz there lived a man whose name was Job. This man was blameless and upright; he feared God and shunned evil. He had seven sons and three daughters, and he owned seven thousand sheep, three thousand camels, five hundred yoke of oxen and five hundred donkeys, and had a large number of servants. He was the greatest man among all the people of the East.
>
> His sons used to take turns holding feasts in their homes, and they would invite their three sisters to eat and drink with them. When a period of feasting had run

its course, Job would send and have them purified. Early in the morning he would sacrifice a burnt offering for each of them, thinking, "Perhaps my children have sinned and cursed God in their hearts." This was Job's regular custom. (1:1–5)

This book is about a relationship between a "real" man and a "real" God. They are who they are. Job was a man who believed in God, and God is not just who Job thought He was. He could not be changed by what Job thought He should be. *God is God.* The story is far from what we would imagine.

One day when Job's sons and daughters were feasting and drinking wine at the oldest brother's house, a messenger came to Job and said, "The oxen were plowing and the donkeys were grazing nearby, and the Sabeans attacked and carried them off. They put the servants to the sword, and I am the only one who has escaped to tell you!"

While he was still speaking, another messenger came and said, "The fire of God fell from the sky and burned up the sheep and the servants, and I am the only one who has escaped to tell you!"

While he was still speaking, another messenger came and said, "The Chaldeans formed three raiding parties and swept down on your camels and carried them off. They put the servants to the sword, and I am the only one who has escaped to tell you!"

While he was still speaking, yet another messenger came and said, "Your sons and daughters were feasting and drinking wine at the oldest brother's house, when suddenly a mighty wind swept in from the desert and struck the four corners of the house. It collapsed on them and they are dead, and I am the only one who has escaped to tell you!" (1:13–19)

So Satan went out from the presence of the Lord and afflicted Job with painful sores from the soles of his feet to the top of his head. (2:7)

His wife said to him, "Are you still holding on to your integrity? Curse God and die!" (2:9)

Why didn't Job just give up? Surely things couldn't get any worse. Can you imagine anything beyond what happened to him? His wife certainly thought the situation was as bad as it could get. She couldn't think of anything left to do but to curse God and die. At least that would end his pain. But Job thought God must know what He was doing. And he couldn't think of anyone other than God who could cause things to happen. Therefore, the story says:

He replied, "You are talking like a foolish woman. Shall we accept good from God, and not trouble?" In all this, Job did not sin in what he said. (2:10)

Even though Job was mistaken about trouble coming from God, because he had been blameless and upright and because he had feared God and shunned evil, somehow a wisdom deep within him knew he could trust God. He did not understand how his devotion to God and his suffering fit together. That is why he longed to talk to God about it. He knew God could explain everything if He just would. So he continued to beg God to give him a hearing. He believed therein was the comfort he longed for.

At certain times each of us must wonder why God doesn't just zap Satan and get it over with. We believe that would comfort us. He certainly has the power to do such a thing. But that is not who God is. Just because Satan rebelled against God and tries to be equal with God and constantly tries to lead others to rebel with him is not reason enough for God to turn his back on Satan. God loves the world. He loved everyone from the beginning and that includes Satan. That love shows in these verses.

One day the angels came to present themselves before the Lord, and *Satan also came* with them. The Lord said to Satan, "Where have you come from?"

Satan answered the Lord, "From roaming through the earth and going back and forth in it." (1:6–7)

On another day the angels came to present themselves before the Lord, and *Satan also came with them to present himself before him*. And the Lord said to Satan, "Where have you come from?"

Satan answered the Lord, "From roaming through the earth and going back and forth in it." (2:1–2)

In reading the following passages, I have been impressed that God was not sicking Satan on Job but was trying to win Satan back from rebellion through Job's example of faith.

Then the Lord said to Satan, "Have you considered my servant Job? There is no one on earth like him; he is blameless and upright, a man who fears God and shuns evil." (1:8)

Then the Lord said to Satan, "Have you considered my servant Job? There is no one on earth like him; he is blameless and upright, a man who fears God and shuns evil. And he still maintains his integrity, though you incited me against him to ruin him without any reason." (2:3)

In his infinite knowledge God knew Satan would not relent, but God must try because that is who He is. As surely as Satan is a deceiver and a liar, he deceives himself as well. And as surely as God is truth and love, He must be true to Himself even when He relates to the evil one.

Satan was sure that he himself was right. He was willing to argue with God, even implying that things appeared as they did because God cheated.

> "Does Job fear God for nothing?" Satan replied. "Have you not put a hedge around him and his household and everything he has? You have blessed the work of his hands, so that his flocks and herds are spread throughout the land. But stretch out your hand and strike everything he has, and he will surely curse you to your face." (1:9–11)

> "Skin for skin!" Satan replied. "A man will give all he has for his own life. But stretch out your hand and strike his flesh and bones, and he will surely curse you to your face." (2:4–5)

How else can God prove that He is right except to allow Satan to try and to fail to prove Him wrong?

> The Lord said to Satan, "Very well, then, everything he has is in your hands, but on the man himself do not lay a finger."

> Then Satan went out from the presence of the Lord. (1:12)

When all Satan's tricks failed and Job remained true to God, he came once again to accuse God of hedging Job in by His admonition to "not lay a finger" on Job.

> The Lord said to Satan, "Very well, then, he is in your hands; but you must spare his life." (2:6)

He allowed Satan to trouble Job, but He set limits on what Satan could do. *The life of Job belonged to God alone.*

Praise God! Even when we think Job was despairing—judging by his interpretation of all these trials—Job and God were winning!

Love,
Sue

Unlike Popular Explanations,
God Is Perfect

Dear Sue,

Your insight into God's relationship with Satan is intriguing. I had never thought about that, but yours does seem to be a plausible explanation, if not the only one. That certainly shows God's never-ending love, even for those whose purpose is to rebel against Him. Job was not a pawn in God's hand nor Satan's, he was a living example of a person who "feared God for nothing" (1:9). That defeats Satan and his theory about people.

The more I come to know Job, the more I appreciate him. He seems to be a "type A" person who liked things organized and ordered.

> "Why does the Almighty not set times for judgment? Why must those who know him look in vain for such days?" (24:1)

He questioned why God didn't establish a regular time for court. He desired to bring his case before God so he could hear God's explanation of his situation.

However, Job was also concerned that justice be done for the sake of all those defenseless widows, orphans, and the poor who had been oppressed.

> "Men move boundary stones; they pasture flocks they have stolen. They drive away the orphan's donkey and take the widow's ox in pledge. They thrust the needy from the path and force all the poor of the land into hiding. Like wild donkeys in the desert, the poor go about their labor of foraging food; the wasteland provides food for their children. They gather fodder in the fields and glean in the vineyards of the wicked. Lacking clothes, they spend the night naked; they have nothing to cover themselves in the cold. They are drenched by mountain rains and hug the rocks for lack of shelter. The fatherless child is snatched from the breast; the infant of the poor is seized for a debt. Lacking clothes, they go about naked; they carry the sheaves, but still go hungry. They crush olives among the terraces; they tread the winepresses, yet suffer thirst. The groans of the dying rise from the city, and the souls of the wounded cry out for help. But God charges no one with wrongdoing." (24:2–12)

This shows how compassionate Job was, as well as his passion for justice.

Surely it was difficult for Job to see those who loved darkness and shunned light go free.

> "There are those who rebel against the light, who do not know its ways or stay in its paths. When daylight is gone, the murderer rises up and kills the poor and needy; in the night he steals forth like a thief. The eye of the adulterer watches for dusk; he thinks, 'No eye will see me,' and he keeps his face concealed. In the dark, men break into houses, but by day they shut themselves in; they want nothing to do with the light. For all of them, deep darkness is their morning; they make friends with the terrors of darkness." (24:13–17)

Oh, he knew they were only "foam on the surface of the water" (24:18) and that they would die and not be remembered.

> "As heat and drought snatch away the melted snow, so the grave snatches away those who have sinned." (24:19)

Job never lost sight of God's control.

> "But God drags away the mighty by his power; though they become established, they have no assurance of life. He may let them rest in a feeling of security, but his eyes are on their ways. For a little while they are exalted, and then they are gone; they are brought low and gathered up like all others; they are cut off like heads of grain." (24:22–24)

Job did not see himself as part of the evil doers. He knew God was just, and he would not be swayed by the traditional, trite responses of his foolish friends.

It is so easy to give in to tradition and popular explanations of how or why things are. I hope we can be strong enough to question the glib answers to life's mysteries and face God in the assurance that He alone is perfectly just and righteous. As we have learned before, may we never forget that God also loves us dearly and has our best interest at heart.

Praise God for the great things He has done!

I love you,
Dick

When the Tried and True Doesn't Work,
Love Holds On

Dearest Dick,

Job was either so sure he was right that he thought no one could prove him wrong. Or he was so unsure that he challenged any and all to debate with him in order that he might find the truth.

> "If this is not so, who can prove me false and reduce my words to nothing?" (24:25)

It is only natural for us to try to solve our problems according to our best knowledge, usually in the same way that our families and friends solve theirs. If something works for others, we expect it to work for us as well. I'm sure that must be why the story relates:

> Then Job took a piece of broken pottery and scraped himself with it as he sat among the ashes. (2:8)

This was probably the common medical practice in Job's day. Today, if we had a festering sore, we would probably go to a doctor. Perhaps, he would lance it with sterile instruments that are designed for just such a purpose. He would probably also prescribe an antibiotic and perhaps a painkiller. And we would expect to begin to improve immediately.

I'm sure Job thought he was doing everything he could possibly do to help his sores to heal. The scraping method had probably worked in every case he knew of, but not this time. We don't really know how long his sickness remained. We do know that ulcers and scabs covered every part of him, and they were so severe that his own wife thought he would be better off dead (2:9). When his friends arrived they could not bear to look at him.

> When they saw him from a distance, they could hardly recognize him; they began to weep aloud, and they tore their robes and sprinkled dust on their heads. (2:12)

Even after they had time to grow accustomed to his disgusting appearance, he begged them to look at him as he spoke.

> "But now be so kind as to look at me." (6:28a)

We can be certain that he was sick for more than a week because his friends had time to hear of his misfortune and arrange to travel together to be at his side. The Scripture records that they then sat silently for a whole week before speaking to him.

> Then they sat on the ground with him for seven days and seven nights. No one said a word to him, because they saw how great his suffering was. (2:13)

Evidently during that week of silence, Job showed no signs of improvement because we read:

> After this, Job opened his mouth and cursed the day of his birth. (3:1)

He poured out the depths of his torment in lamenting that he was ever born.

> "May the day of my birth perish, and the night it was said, 'A boy is born!' That day—may it turn to darkness; may God above not care about it; may no light shine upon it. May darkness and deep shadow claim it once more; may a cloud settle over it; may blackness overwhelm its light. That night—may thick darkness seize it; may it not be included among the days of the year nor be entered in any of the months. May that night be barren; may no shout of joy be heard in it. May those who curse days curse that day, those who are ready to rouse Leviathan. May its morning stars become dark; may it wait for daylight in vain and not see the first rays of dawn, for it did not shut the doors of the womb on me to hide trouble from my eyes.

> "Why did I not perish at birth, and die as I came from the womb? Why were there knees to receive me and breasts that I might be nursed? For now I would be lying down in peace; I would be asleep and at rest with kings and counselors of the earth, who built for themselves places now lying in ruins, with rulers who had gold, who filled their houses with silver. Or why was I not hidden in the ground like a stillborn child, like an infant who never saw the light of day? There the wicked cease from turmoil, and there the weary are at rest. Captives also enjoy their ease; they no longer hear the slave driver's shout. The small and the great are there, and the slave is freed from his master.

> "Why is light given to those in misery, and life to the bitter of soul, to those who long for death that does not come, who search for it more than for hidden treasure, who are filled with gladness and rejoice when they reach the grave? Why is life given to a man whose way is hidden, whom God has hedged in? For sighing comes to me instead of food; my groans pour out like water. What I feared has come upon me; what I dreaded has happened to me. I have no peace, no quietness; I have no rest, but only turmoil." (3:3–26)

(It seems strange to me that Satan would have accused God of putting a hedge around Job and his household and everything he had to protect him from evil in 1:10. God allowed Satan to ruin Job, so where is that protective hedge? Then in the situation above, Job is accusing God of putting a hedge around him to prevent him from finding his way to happiness. God gets blamed no matter what.)

Job's sickness must have gone on for at least several months because in chapter 7 he referred to:

> ". . . months of futility, and nights of misery . . . assigned to me." (7:3)

There was nothing more his friends could suggest that he do. They had never been as sick and never experienced such pain as he. So they turned their attention to the reason he had become so ill in the first place. They could only conclude that he must have done something really bad. Eliphaz began to argue almost immediately:

> "Consider now: Who, being innocent, has ever perished? Where were the upright ever destroyed? As I have observed, those who plow evil and those who sow trouble reap it." (4:7–8)

They were completely confused by his refusal to repent. Certainly if Eliphaz, Bildad, or Zophar had been sick, they would have known it was because of their sin, and they would have been quick to repent and let the healing begin!

Only you know how many of our friends have been just as confounded by me. They just can't understand why a doctor could not merely examine me, tell me what is wrong, prescribe some medicine, and I would be well the next week. Life has always worked that way for them. Why should I be different?

Most people have never had a disease that was difficult for doctors to diagnose and treat. I can't count the numerous diseases friends have suggested I might have (as if the doctors had not already tested for everything they could imagine). Only occasionally someone has given me valuable information that my doctor had not yet considered. Some of my friends have never had a reaction to a medication and can't comprehend my fear after reacting to many different drugs, both prescription and nonprescription. Those who want so much to help can't believe that a pain pill that relieves them thoroughly could cause such havoc in me. So why should we expect them to understand?

Yet, like Job, I have been unable to resist trying to explain my malady in hopes of increasing their sympathy. But, alas, instead of helping them to understand how I feel, I have only inadvertently invited their inadequate advice (and their indifference to me)—and the emotional pain that comes with it.

I thank God that He has given you to walk beside me. I know that it has not been easy. I *am* rather odd. Unlike me, you have had a rather straightforward medical history. I am glad for you. But that has made it extra hard to sympathize with me sometimes. I accept that. However, you have kept on trying to demystify this strange woman you married. Thanks. You're getting better and better at it as the years go by. Even if you are the only human being who ever understands me, that is enough. Thanks for not saying, "Why don't you just curse God and die!"

I love you so much,
Sue

LETTER 18

*When "Traditional Medicine" Doesn't Fit,
True Faith Doesn't Compromise*

Dearest Sue,

Yes, the world operates on the premise that we are all pretty much "normal." (Look how close that is to Norma, your first name—I guess Normal Sue wouldn't quite fit. Ha!) I know how you long to be like everyone else so you can be treated with modern medicine instead of reacting to so many different drugs. I know that has been a true "thorn in your flesh." However, I admire the way you have handled this thorn, including the emotional pain caused by sincere but insensitive friends. I trust God will continue to help me be even more empathetic.

In Bildad's brief statement, mankind was on the lowest rung of the ladder.

> "Dominion and awe belong to God; he establishes order in the heights of heaven. Can his forces be numbered? Upon whom does his light not rise? How then can a man be righteous before God? How can one born of woman be pure? If even the moon is not bright and the stars are not pure in his eyes, how much less man, who is but a maggot—a son of man, who is only a worm!" (25:2–6)

He gave evidence of having an exalted view of God, but there his wisdom ceased. Like many today, Bildad saw people as *totally* depraved. He seemed to believe that people were not capable of any righteousness. They could never be pure. How tragic that he should consider God's creation as a "maggot" or "worm." This is certainly a contrast to Psalm 8:4–6.

Job understood the true impact of Bildad's remarks and made fun of his view of man.

> "How you have helped the powerless! How you have saved the arm that is feeble! What advice you have offered to one without wisdom! And what great insight you have displayed! Who has helped you utter these words? And whose spirit spoke from your mouth?" (26:2–4)

He went on to write of God's majesty shown in nature:

> "He spreads out the northern skies over empty space; he suspends the earth over nothing. He wraps up the waters in his clouds, yet the clouds do not burst under their weight. He covers the face of the full moon, spreading his clouds over it. He marks out the horizon on the face of the waters for a boundary between light and darkness. The pillars of the heavens quake, aghast at his rebuke. By his power he churned up the sea; by his wisdom he cut Rahab to pieces. By his breath the skies became fair; his hand pierced the gliding serpent. And these are but the outer fringe of his works; how faint the whisper we hear of him! Who then can understand the thunder of his power?" (26:7–14)

I especially like the phrase, "And these are but the outer fringe of his works" (verse 14a); Job realized we cannot comprehend all there is to know about God.

However, Job rebutted Bildad's charge that no one could be pure or righteous. Job had demonstrated his integrity in his life:

> ". . . as long as I have life within me, the breath of God in my nostrils, my lips will not speak wickedness, and my tongue will utter no deceit. I will never admit you are in the right; till I die, I will not deny my integrity. I will maintain my righteousness and never let go of it; my conscience will not reproach me as long as I live." (27:3–6)

He agreed with his friends that God does judge the wicked and none escape. He declared:

> "For what hope has the godless when he is cut off, when God takes away his life? Does God listen to his cry when distress comes upon him? Will he find delight in the Almighty? Will he call upon God at all times?

"I will teach you about the power of God; the ways of the Almighty I will not conceal. You have all seen this yourselves. Why then this meaningless talk?

"Here is the fate God allots to the wicked, the heritage a ruthless man receives from the Almighty: However many his children, their fate is the sword; his offspring will never have enough to eat. The plague will bury those who survive him, and their widows will not weep for them. Though he heaps up silver like dust and clothes like piles of clay, what he lays up the righteous will wear, and the innocent will divide his silver. The house he builds is like a moth's cocoon, like a hut made by a watchman. He lies down wealthy, but will do so no more; when he opens his eyes, all is gone. Terrors overtake him like a flood; a tempest snatches him away in the night. The east wind carries him off, and he is gone; it sweeps him out of his place. It hurls itself against him without mercy as he flees headlong from its power. It claps its hands in derision and hisses him out of his place." (27:8–23)

Although he believed the wicked are without hope (27:8), Job did not believe he was an evildoer or one of the "godless." He would not accept the "normal" explanation for things. The traditional "medicine" just did not work on him. He knew that God would hear him eventually. But even if He didn't, Job would remain true to God and never curse Him, as his wife suggested.

"You gotta like this guy!" He wasn't perfect and he knew that, but he also knew that he was basically righteous. But the greatest thing about Job to me is his uncompromising faith in God.

Love,
Dick

LETTER 19

Not All Wicked Men Suffer, and Not All Those Who Suffer Are Wicked

Dearest Dick,

I agree that Job shared the view that God does and should punish the wicked. Job sounded like the Psalmist when he said:

"May my enemies be like the wicked, my adversaries like the unjust!" (27:7)

It is obvious in this statement that Job did not consider himself wicked. Remember the arguments of Job's friends that the wicked always suffer; therefore, those who suffer must be wicked. Eliphaz said:

"He [God] thwarts the plans of the crafty, so that their hands achieve no success. He catches the wise in their craftiness, and the schemes of the wily are swept away. Darkness comes upon them in the daytime; at noon they grope as in the night. He saves the needy from the sword in their mouth; he saves them from the clutches of the powerful. So the poor have hope, and injustice shuts its mouth." (5:12–16)

Bildad continued with the same idea but expanded it to say that if Job were righteous he would be showered with blessings.

"How long will you say such things? Your words are a blustering wind. Does God pervert justice? Does the Almighty pervert what is right? When your children sinned against him, he gave them over to the penalty of their sin. But if you will look to God and plead with the Almighty, if you are pure and upright, even now he will rouse himself on your behalf and restore you to your rightful place. Your beginnings will seem humble, so prosperous will your future be." (8:2–7)

They argued that not only does God make sure the wicked suffer but He also will ensure that the righteous do not. They appealed to the learning of their forefathers for proof that the way of the wicked is confounded. Bildad said:

"Ask the former generations and find out what their fathers learned, for we were born only yesterday and know nothing, and our days on earth are but a shadow. Will they not instruct you and tell you? Will they not bring forth words from their understanding?" (8:8–10)

Their traditions said that man could not prosper apart from God; therefore, the man who was cut off from God by his unrighteousness must suffer. If they saw a man suffering, they concluded that he must have committed some act that separated him from God. Bildad illustrated how mankind had reasoned and arrived at this point:

"Can papyrus grow tall where there is no marsh? Can reeds thrive without water? While still growing and uncut, they wither more quickly than grass. Such is the destiny of all who forget God; so perishes the hope of the godless. What he trusts in is fragile; what he relies on is a spider's web. He leans on his web, but it gives way; he clings to it, but it does not hold. He is like a well-watered plant in the sunshine, spreading its shoots over the garden; it entwines its roots around a pile of rocks and looks for a place among the stones. But when it is torn from its spot, that place disowns it and says, 'I never saw you.' Surely its life withers away, and from the soil other plants grow." (8:11–19)

Job answered that God does not draw such a distinct line between the wicked and the righteous. He was willing to risk his life to state what he believed. What did he have to lose?

"Although I am blameless, I have no concern for myself; I despise my own life. It is all the same; that is why I say, 'He destroys both the blameless and the wicked.' When a scourge brings sudden death, he mocks the despair of the innocent. When a land falls into the hands of the wicked, he blindfolds its judges. If it is not he, then who is it?" (9:21–24)

Job knew from his own observations that not all wicked men live a troubled life.

"Men at ease have contempt for misfortune as the fate of those whose feet are slipping. The tents of marauders are undisturbed, and those who provoke God are secure—those who carry their god in their hands." (12:5–6)

He called on nature itself as a witness that God treats all humankind as He pleases without discrimination.

"But ask the animals, and they will teach you, or the birds of the air, and they will tell you; or speak to the earth, and it will teach you, or let the fish of the sea inform you. Which of all these does not know that the hand of the Lord has done this? In his hand is the life of every creature and the breath of all mankind." (12:7–10)

Unless we look closely, in chapter 27 Job seemed to contradict what he had said in chapters 9 and 12. However, in these early chapters, he was arguing about the quality of the wicked's life on earth, and in chapter 27 he was talking about what would happen to the wicked when they died.

Job was sure that he was not suffering as a direct result of his wickedness. That is why he continued to contend for his right to question the Almighty. When I have been unable to see any reason for my own suffering, I also have wanted an explanation from God. I think that is only natural.

Love,
Sue

LETTER 20

*Our Explanations Are Empty;
God's Wisdom Stands Alone*

Dearest Sue,

When we are not wise enough to discern an answer to life's mysteries, we must trust God. We do not live long enough to understand the perplexities of life. God does not always reveal answers to us, perhaps because we can't understand or because we are not yet ready to understand. Therefore, we must simply trust God, knowing that He loves us and always desires His best for us.

People have always boasted about their wisdom. I'm sure this was true in Job's day. Job painted an interesting picture of man's search for wisdom.

> "There is a mine for silver and a place where gold is refined. Iron is taken from the earth, and copper is smelted from ore. Man puts an end to the darkness; he searches the farthest recesses for ore in the blackest darkness. Far from where people dwell he cuts a shaft, in places forgotten by the foot of man; far from men he dangles and sways. The earth, from which food comes, is transformed below as by fire; sapphires come from its rocks, and its dust contains nuggets of gold. No bird of prey knows that hidden path, no falcon's eye has seen it. Proud beasts do not set foot on it, and no lion prowls there. Man's hand assaults the flinty rock and lays bare the roots of the mountains. He tunnels through the rock; his eyes see all its treasures. He searches the sources of the rivers and brings hidden things to light." (28:1–11)

This is an amazing description of early mining technology. I had never realized such methods were known in ancient days.

However, despite man's advanced technology, he still does not know wisdom. Regardless of where we look or how much we're prepared to pay, true knowledge eludes us. Job continued by asking:

> "But where can wisdom be found? Where does understanding dwell? Man does not comprehend its worth; it cannot be found in the land of the living." (28:12–13)

Job mentioned many valuable stones in verses 14–19 but said that even the most valuable of these cannot purchase wisdom.

> "It is hidden from the eyes of every living thing. . . . God understands the way to it and he alone knows where it dwells. . . ." (28:21a, 23)

Only God understands wisdom or knows all the answers:

> "for he views the ends of the earth and sees everything under the heavens." (28:24)

When God defined wisdom for man, He didn't actually define it. Rather He told us the importance of trusting God and turning away from the one who would lead us to distrust Him, the evil tempter, Satan.

"The fear of the Lord—that is wisdom, and to shun evil is understanding."
(28:28b)

The fear of the Lord is so much more important than we realize. It means that
we respect God so much and revere him to such an extent that we can trust
Him with everything. This is why Job could say:

"Though he slay me, yet will I hope in him. . . ." (13:15a)

What a tremendous lesson in *real faith!* Adversity backs us against a wall
where we have no other resources; we're at the end of our rope. Sadly, it often
takes that for us to realize the frailty and emptiness of human explanation.
We simply thrust ourselves on God and have *full confidence* that He will do
the "right" thing. He will give us what is best for us and for fulfilling His
purpose. He has the long look and knows how it's all going to end. This
causes me to want to trust Him more completely. This is awesome!
Hallelujah, what a Savior!

I love you,
Dick

LETTER 21

When Life Drives Us Out on a Limb,
Belief in Our Integrity Is Comforting

Dearest Dick,

How beautiful is your faith! Trusting seems to come so easily for you. I love
you for that, but I have also often been jealous of you. I know you would say
that your faith is sometimes weak as well. But you don't stay out there on a
limb "forever" like I sometimes do.

I have wanted you, even sometimes begged you, to get me off my limb, but I
didn't know how to ask, and you didn't know how to give. Only God knows
how much we wanted to. I guess that just proves that a person's faith is his
or hers alone.

I have often regretted that I seem to have to question everything as far as I
can push it to come up with the same answer: simply trust Him. I yearn to

know that what I believe about life is based on what God has revealed to me through my own personal encounter with Him. Often that leads me far afield from human explanations. Most of my life has been spent dangling at the end of that rope.

I guess that's why I was a philosophy major in college. I was always amused when anyone asked, "Who is your favorite philosopher?" in much the same way they would ask, "Who is your favorite author?" I never had a favorite philosopher or author. Each one could show me his method of asking questions, but to have declared a favorite would have implied that I agreed with his answers. *My answers* must be my own! That's who I am!

I know that fact has really frustrated you at times. I am sorry. I just can't seem to help being like I am. Thank you and thank God for not giving up on me.

I am so grateful that God chose to work in the life of a man like Job and that He caused someone to record that relationship. Job was a lot like you—a righteous man who prayed daily for his children. But then, it seemed like everything was gone! It must have been hard for Job to understand enough to talk about it. Sometimes he must have been confounded by his own words, but God continued to guide him.

It makes me sad to think that so few have understood what God was trying to tell us through Job. You know how I have cried when I believed that God had revealed something to me and I could find no effective way to share that truth.

However, it is so much easier to read or sing or talk about whatever everybody else is reading or singing or talking about. There is comfort in being part of a crowd. We haven't changed much since Job's day. As Eliphaz said, we believe that:

> "He [God] performs wonders that cannot be fathomed, miracles that cannot be counted. He bestows rain on the earth; he sends water upon the countryside." (5:9–10)

And we also want to believe:

> "The lowly he sets on high, and those who mourn are lifted to safety." (5:11)

But at times some of us don't experience life that way. We have trouble ourselves believing our intense pain goes on and on, let alone explaining it to someone else. Listen to Job.

"If only my anguish could be weighed and all my misery be placed on the scales! It would surely outweigh the sand of the seas—no wonder my words have been impetuous. The arrows of the Almighty are in me, my spirit drinks in their poison; God's terrors are marshaled against me. Does a wild donkey bray when it has grass, or an ox bellow when it has fodder? Is tasteless food eaten without salt, or is there flavor in the white of an egg? I refuse to touch it; such food makes me ill.

"Oh, that I might have my request, that God would grant what I hope for, that God would be willing to crush me, to let loose his hand and cut me off! Then I would still have this consolation—my joy in unrelenting pain—that I had not denied the words of the Holy One.

"What strength do I have, that I should still hope? What prospects, that I should be patient? Do I have the strength of stone? Is my flesh bronze? Do I have any power to help myself, now that success has been driven from me?" (6:2–13)

Sometimes Job was so desperate that he just needed his friends to assure him that he was not crazy—that pursuing a hearing with God was not out of the question. But his friends failed miserably. Hear Job's cry:

"A despairing man should have the devotion of his friends, even though he forsakes the fear of the Almighty. But my brothers are as undependable as intermittent streams, as the streams that overflow when darkened by thawing ice and swollen with melting snow, but that cease to flow in the dry season, and in the heat vanish from their channels. Caravans turn aside from their routes; they go up into the wasteland and perish. The caravans of Tema look for water, the traveling merchants of Sheba look in hope. They are distressed, because they had been confident; they arrive there, only to be disappointed. Now you too have proved to be of no help; you see something dreadful and are afraid. Have I ever said, 'Give something on my behalf, pay a ransom for me from your wealth, deliver me from the hand of the enemy, ransom me from the clutches of the ruthless'?" (6:14–23)

Sounds familiar, doesn't it? Thank you for crying with me when no one else wanted to try to understand. That is true love! How fortunate I am! And thank you for the many times you have assured me that I am not crazy.

Perhaps the reason "You gotta like this guy" is because you've been living with someone for so many years who in some ways is a lot like him. I am so very grateful that you have not given up on me! Even when I am so very different from you, you keep trying to understand!

Your loving wife,
Sue

When Life Can't Be Like It Used to Be, Make the Most of Life As It Is

Darling Sue,

Yes, we are two different people. It probably would be dull if we were the same. Sometimes I have felt like I should question more and that has stretched my understanding and helped me grow. Your questions, when not intimidating, help me to gain insight. I'm thankful you appreciate my ability to believe, but I need your questions lest I take things only at face value. That's what makes us a team!

Yes, Job needed someone to understand him and to sympathize with him. Unfortunately his wife and friends refused to love him enough or to give him enough credit to believe his words. He had established an outstanding record, and he longed to go back to those days when he was respected. He knew that God's "lamp shone upon" his head and "God's intimate friendship blessed" his house (29:3–4). You can almost see Job in his "heyday" before the tragedy.

> "When I went to the gate of the city and took my seat in the public square, the young men saw me and stepped aside and the old men rose to their feet; the chief men refrained from speaking and covered their mouths with their hands; the voices of the nobles were hushed, and their tongues stuck to the roof of their mouths. Whoever heard me spoke well of me, and those who saw me commended me, because I rescued the poor who cried for help, and the fatherless who had none to assist him. The man who was dying blessed me; I made the widow's heart sing. I put on righteousness as my clothing; justice was my robe and my turban. I was eyes to the blind and feet to the lame. I was a father to the needy; I took up the case of the stranger. I broke the fangs of the wicked and snatched the victims from their teeth." (29:7–17)

Job was a man of great influence; his life and words helped many.

> "Men listened to me expectantly, waiting in silence for my counsel. After I had spoken, they spoke no more; my words fell gently on their ears. They waited for me as for showers and drank in my words as the spring rain. When I smiled at them, they scarcely believed it; the light of my face was precious to them. I chose the way for them and sat as their chief; I dwelt as a king among his troops; I was like one who comforts mourners." (29:21–25)

When life is going well we anticipate that it will continue that way until we die. That was certainly what Job believed.

> "I thought, 'I will die in my own house, my days as numerous as the grains of sand.'" (29:18)

When adversity comes, we naturally think of good times and long to return. I remember thinking in Zambia that we would one day retire from missions. Even when you didn't recover and we moved here, we expected to return someday.

Now, we face a new challenge. It probably will not necessitate a move, but it does require some adjustments. We both still long for life the way it used to be. However, there is also the challenge to make the most of life as it is. I know God isn't finished with us yet. I look forward to continuing to team up with you so we can be available for what God wants to do through us. I love you so much!

Your loving husband,
Dick

LETTER 23

When Hope Dies, the Touch of Another
Can Rekindle the Flame

Dearest Dick,

I too believed that death would come quickly at the end of a long and happy life. Job's words reflect my dreams as well.

> "My roots will reach to the water, and the dew will lie all night on my branches. My glory will remain fresh in me, the bow ever new in my hand." (29:19–20)

I know now, that will not necessarily be true. Some of us do suffer for a long time before we die. But that doesn't have to be the end of the story. No matter what my physical circumstances, when we are a team, I am happy. When we are teaming up under God's directives, I am happiest. It seems that, no matter how intense my pain, sharing a project with you always helps. Perhaps, that is why I protest so furiously when you get involved in projects of your own and I can't help you.

At times I have been so without energy, both physical and mental, that I just didn't have the power to begin much under my own steam. But if you provided the initiative and if you offered the coattail, I was glad to grab hold and come along.

I can identify with Job's day (and night) that he described in chapter 7.

"Does not man have hard service on earth? Are not his days like those of a hired man? Like a slave longing for the evening shadows, or a hired man waiting eagerly for his wages, so I have been allotted months of futility, and nights of misery have been assigned to me. When I lie down I think, 'How long before I get up?' The night drags on, and I toss till dawn. My body is clothed with worms and scabs, my skin is broken and festering.

"My days are swifter than a weaver's shuttle, and they come to an end without hope. Remember, O God, that my life is but a breath; my eyes will never see happiness again. The eye that now sees me will see me no longer; you will look for me, but I will be no more. As a cloud vanishes and is gone, so he who goes down to the grave does not return. He will never come to his house again; his place will know him no more.

"Therefore I will not keep silent; I will speak out in the anguish of my spirit, I will complain in the bitterness of my soul. Am I the sea, or the monster of the deep, that you put me under guard? When I think my bed will comfort me and my couch will ease my complaint, even then you frighten me with dreams and terrify me with visions, so that I prefer strangling and death, rather than this body of mine. I despise my life; I would not live forever. Let me alone; my days have no meaning." (7:1–16)

Job must have thought his friends didn't appreciate the intensity of his distress. He tried again in his next speech to describe his lack of joy.

"My days are swifter than a runner; they fly away without a glimpse of joy. They skim past like boats of papyrus, like eagles swooping down on their prey." (9:25–26)

I have had days that drag on and I seem to accomplish very little. Other days slide to an end, and I feel completely useless. When night comes, I toss and turn until almost dawn. Finally I fall asleep and have some really weird nightmare. Where is the hope when these days and nights turn into months or even years? Can one who lives this way be blamed for thinking death might be better?

Like Job, I have to keep on kicking. Can't God work even this for good? When will He begin to make sense of it all?

Hanging onto your coattail and looking through you, I can see a glimmer of light. Thank you for your faith in God and your faith in me when my own faith is just a sputtering flicker. Being on your team is sparking that flicker into a flame once again.

Love,
Sue

LETTER 24

Can Any Person Comfort One
Who Feels Mocked by Life?

Dear Sue,

As I read the thirtieth chapter, I realized again that I have great difficulty identifying with Job's misery and forsaken condition. He felt totally rejected by everyone, there was no one to comfort him.

> "But now they mock me, men younger that I, whose fathers I would have disdained to put with my sheep dogs. Of what use was the strength of their hands to me, since their vigor had gone from them? Haggard from want and hunger, they roamed the parched land in desolate wastelands at night. In the brush they gathered salt herbs, and their food was the root of the broom tree. They were banished from their fellow men, shouted at as if they were thieves. They were forced to live in the dry stream beds, among the rocks and in holes in the ground. They brayed among the bushes and huddled in the undergrowth. A base and nameless brood, they were driven out of the land.
>
> "And now their sons mock me in song; I have become a byword among them. They detest me and keep their distance; they do not hesitate to spit in my face. Now that God has unstrung my bow and afflicted me, they throw off restraint in my presence. On my right the tribe attacks; they lay snares for my feet, they build their siege ramps against me. They break up my road; they succeed in destroying me—without anyone's helping them. They advance as through a gaping breach; amid the ruins they come rolling in. Terrors overwhelm me; my dignity is driven away as by the wind, my safety vanishes like a cloud." (30:1–15)

That must have been a devastating feeling. There have been a few times in my life when I felt alone but nothing the way Job felt.

Not only was he alone, but his pain was so intense he could not describe it.

> "And now my life ebbs away; days of suffering grip me. Night pierces my bones; my gnawing pains never rest. . . . The churning inside me never stops; days of suffering confront me." (30:16–17, 27)

Here again I find it difficult to imagine such pain because my own experience has not included such. I'm thankful that I have been spared, but I certainly can't say, "I know how you feel."

Since I have not had such experiences (shall I say "yet"), I hope that my sympathy soothes to some limited extent. I want so much to be able to comfort you, but it is so hard from my own experience to find just the right words to say.

I love you,
Dick

LETTER 25

Prolonged Pain Precipitates Hard Questions
Demanding to Be Heard

Dearest Dick,

Please don't feel that you must eventually bear "your share of pain"—that equal suffering is the inevitable for all. I don't believe the Bible teaches us that. And I certainly pray that you may never suffer extreme pain, even though I know that you too have aches at times.

I don't think Job believed that all should suffer like he was, although he wished to be without suffering. Neither did Job hold that all suffering is in direct proportion to one's sin nor freedom from pain is weighed by one's righteousness.

> "Can anyone teach knowledge to God, since he judges even the highest? One man dies in full vigor, completely secure and at ease, his body well nourished, his bones rich with marrow. Another man dies in bitterness of soul, never having

enjoyed anything good. Side by side they lie in the dust, and worms cover them both." (21:22–26)

In fact, in my opinion, the only role pain plays in the drama of Job is to cause him to beg for explanation from God. He asked,

"Is my complaint directed to man? Why should I not be impatient?" (21:4)

"In his great power God becomes like clothing to me; he binds me like the neck of my garment. He throws me into the mud, and I am reduced to dust and ashes.

"I cry out to you, O God, but you do not answer; I stand up, but you merely look at me. You turn on me ruthlessly; with the might of your hand you attack me. You snatch me up and drive me before the wind; you toss me about in the storm. I know you will bring me down to death, to the place appointed for all the living.

"Surely no one lays a hand on a broken man when he cries for help in his distress. Have I not wept for those in trouble? Has not my soul grieved for the poor? Yet when I hoped for good, evil came; when I looked for light, then came darkness. . . . I go about blackened, but not by the sun; I stand up in the assembly and cry for help. I have become a brother of jackals, a companion of owls. My skin grows black and peels; my body burns with fever. My harp is tuned to mourning, and my flute to the sound of wailing." (30:18–26, 28–31)

". . . if the men of my household have never said, 'Who has not had his fill of Job's meat?'—but no stranger had to spend the night in the street, for my door was always open to the traveler. . . ." (31:31–32)

I too have wondered why, if I had shown mercy to those in distress, God would not send someone to comfort me. I too have found that the songs which poured from my heart were always in a minor key.

Job didn't expect answers to his questions from man, although it may appear so. Even if another had sat beside him in those ashes and shared the agony of the scraping sherd, Job would not have called on that one for identification with his plight. That was impossible. All he seemed to want from those around him was that they listen without questioning to what he felt he must say.

"Listen carefully to my words; let this be the consolation you give me." (21:2)

His arguments were opposed to theirs. But was his pain the cause for that? I don't think so. I think these ideas were forming inside Job even when he was the healthiest, wealthiest man in the East. But it was the *impatience* he found in his illness that spurred him to demand answers from the Almighty. The inconsistencies of life didn't agitate him so much before. The inconsistency of his illness agitated him day and night. He sought release in acceptance of his ideas. He wanted an affirmative answer from both the Almighty and from his friends to his question, "Now, have I got this figured out right?"

How funny that we refer to the "patience of Job." He may not have felt patient at all!

Love,
Sue

When You Can't Give Up,
How Can You Remain Humble?

Dearest Sue,

I guess patience is the real issue most of us face. It is so closely related to faith. While Job seemed to hold on to his faith in God, he certainly was impatient with God for not answering him. So in one way, he is a good example of a man of faith, while at the same time, he was unable to find "rest" for his anxious spirit.

But would Job have ever stood up to his friends and their traditional explanations of life if he had not argued with them? Somehow it is difficult to see Job just sitting in his ashes, scraping his body with a sherd and calmly saying, "I just believe everything is going to be fine, I love God and He loves me."

As a child, I thought there was no place to hide from God. I wondered how He could see me in a closet. Job knew that God saw his every move.

> "For what is man's lot from God above, his heritage from the Almighty on high? Is it not ruin for the wicked, disaster for those who do wrong? Does he not see my ways and count my every step?" (31:2–4)

I also see Job as a responsible man who respected others who were made in the image of God, just as he was. He had a high ethic, and his reason for being ethical was that he was a *good* man. He always tried to avoid unethical ways.

> "I made a covenant with my eyes not to look lustfully at a girl." (31:1)

"If I have walked in falsehood or my foot has hurried after deceit—let God weigh me in honest scales and he will know that I am blameless—if my steps have turned from the path, if my heart has been led by my eyes, or if my hands have been defiled, then may others eat what I have sown, and may my crops be uprooted.

"If my heart has been enticed by a woman, or if I have lurked at my neighbor's door, then may my wife grind another man's grain, and may other men sleep with her. For that would have been shameful, a sin to be judged. It is a fire that burns to Destruction; it would have uprooted my harvest.

"If I have denied justice to my menservants and maidservants when they had a grievance against me, what will I do when God confronts me? What will I answer when called to account? Did not he who made me in the womb make them? Did not the same one form us both within our mothers?" (31:5–15)

However, Job also believed that if he were evil, God would punish him.

"If I have denied the desires of the poor or let the eyes of the widow grow weary, if I have kept my bread to myself, not sharing it with the fatherless—but from my youth I reared him as would a father, and from my birth I guided the widow—if I have seen anyone perishing for lack of clothing, or a needy man without a garment, and his heart did not bless me for warming him with the fleece from my sheep, if I have raised my hand against the fatherless, knowing that I had influence in court, then let my arm fall from the shoulder, let it be broken off at the joint. For I dreaded destruction from God, and for fear of his splendor I could not do such things." (31:16–23)

Job's righteousness even included concern for his enemies.

"If I have rejoiced at my enemy's misfortune or gloated over the trouble that came to him—I have not allowed my mouth to sin by invoking a curse against his life—" (31:29–30)

And he had concern for the environment, God's creation.

". . . if my land cries out against me and all its furrows are wet with tears, if I have devoured its yield without payment or broken the spirit of its tenants, then let briers come up instead of wheat and weeds instead of barley." (31:38–40a)

Job was true to God, never turning aside to idolatry.

"If I have put my trust in gold or said to pure gold, 'You are my security,' if I have rejoiced over my great wealth, the fortune my hands had gained, if I have regarded the sun in its radiance or the moon moving in splendor, so that my heart was secretly enticed and my hand offered them a kiss of homage, then these also would be sins to be judged, for I would have been unfaithful to God on high." (31:24–28)

But Job couldn't find comfort! He desperately wanted to talk with God.

("Oh, that I had someone to hear me! I sign now my defense—let the Almighty answer me; let my accuser put his indictment in writing. Surely I would wear it on my shoulder, I would put it on like a crown. I would give him an account of my every step; like a prince I would approach him.") (31:35–37)

Job actually wanted to stand before God and address Him "like a prince." Is there a need for humility here? Impatience can lead us there, can't it?

I love you,
Dick

LETTER 27

God Doesn't Fit Anybody's Mold—
He Is Who HE IS

Dearest Dick,

Ouch! How many times have I been impatient to make you understand some "wonderful" insight and, without my noticing, humility flew out the window and I just became overbearing! If I can do that with you, I know I can do it with God.

Thank goodness God doesn't need my ideas of how things ought to be. He is who "He Is." He is not who we think He is. If He were, Bildad would have been right when he said:

"Surely God does not reject a blameless man or strengthen the hands of evildoers. He will yet fill your mouth with laughter and your lips with shouts of joy. Your enemies will be clothed in shame, and the tents of the wicked will be no more." (8:20–22)

If God were in our image, Zophar's ideas would rule the universe.

"Yet if you devote your heart to him and stretch out your hands to him, if you put away the sin that is in your hand and allow no evil to dwell in your tent, then you will lift up your face without shame; you will stand firm and without fear. You will surely forget your trouble, recalling it only as waters gone by. Life will be brighter than noonday, and darkness will become like morning. You will be secure, because there is hope; you will look about you and take your rest in safety. You will lie down, with no one to make you afraid, and many will court your favor. But the eyes of the wicked will fail, and escape will elude them; their hope will become a dying gasp." (11:13–20)

If God were who Eliphaz thought He was, we could trust his description as the lot of every wicked man on earth.

"Listen to me and I will explain to you; let me tell you what I have seen, what wise men have declared, hiding nothing received from their fathers (to whom alone the land was given when no alien passed among them): All his days the wicked man suffers torment, the ruthless through all the years stored up for him. Terrifying sounds fill his ears; when all seems well, marauders attack him. He despairs of escaping the darkness; he is marked for the sword. He wanders about—food for vultures; he knows the day of darkness is at hand. Distress and anguish fill him with terror; they overwhelm him, like a king poised to attack, because he shakes his fist at God and vaunts himself against the Almighty, defiantly charging against him with a thick, strong shield.

"Though his face is covered with fat and his waist bulges with flesh, he will inhabit ruined towns and houses where no one lives, houses crumbling to rubble. He will no longer be rich and his wealth will not endure, nor will his possessions spread over the land. He will not escape the darkness; a flame will wither his shoots, and the breath of God's mouth will carry him away. Let him not deceive himself by trusting what is worthless, for he will get nothing in return. Before his time he will be paid in full, and his branches will not flourish. He will be like a vine stripped of its unripe grapes, like an olive tree shedding its blossoms. For the company of the godless will be barren, and fire will consume the tents of those who love bribes. They conceive trouble and give birth to evil; their womb fashions deceit." (15:17–35)

All their arguments sounded so good, but the Lord Himself said to Eliphaz:

"I am angry with you and your two friends, because you have not spoken of me what is right, as my servant Job has." (42:7b)

We have heard people say, "My God wouldn't . . ." Or we have been part of expecting God to repeat what we have attributed to Him in the past. That must not be what He means by unchanging. Haven't we learned anything from fingerprints or DNA or just by observing the flowers and the trees and the birds and even the rocks? Everything under the sun is different, and God made it all. He doesn't have to fit into a mold.

> ". . . how faint the whisper we hear of him! Who then can understand the thunder of his power?" (26:14)

Thanks be to God who is not conceived by man. If He were, we would all be doomed by our own wickedness. He is only "I AM." We can't and shouldn't desire to change that.

Love,
Sue

LETTER 28

God Speaks to Us in the Midst
of Many Circumstances

Dearest Sue,

That brings us to Elihu! He was obviously very proud and arrogant, yet he did speak words of wisdom. He seemed to have waited patiently, hoping that the elders would present his argument, but none of them did.

> "They are dismayed and have no more to say; words have failed them. Must I wait, now that they are silent, now that they stand there with no reply? I too will have my say; I too will tell what I know. For I am full of words, and the spirit within me compels me; inside I am like bottled-up wine, like new wineskins ready to burst. I must speak and find relief; I must open my lips and reply." (32:15–20)

Elihu's first message was one that Job and his friends needed to hear, although it didn't really bring comfort to Job. His message was that God speaks to man in the midst of many different circumstances, including calamity.

> "But I tell you, in this you are not right, for God is greater than man. Why do you complain to him that he answers none of man's words? For God does speak—now one way, now another—though man may not perceive it. In a dream, in a

vision of the night, when deep sleep falls on men as they slumber in their beds, he may speak in their ears and terrify them with warnings, to turn man from wrongdoing and keep him from pride, to preserve his soul from the pit, his life from perishing by the sword. Or a man may be chastened on a bed of pain with constant distress in his bones, so that his very being finds food repulsive and his soul loathes the choicest meal. His flesh wastes away to nothing, and his bones, once hidden, now stick out. His soul draws near to the pit, and his life to the messengers of death.

"Yet if there is an angel on his side as a mediator, one out of a thousand, to tell a man what is right for him, to be gracious to him and say, 'Spare him from going down to the pit; I have found a ransom for him'—then his flesh is renewed like a child's; it is restored as in the days of his youth. He prays to God and finds favor with him, he sees God's face and shouts for joy; he is restored by God to his righteous state. Then he comes to men and says, 'I sinned, and perverted what was right, but I did not get what I deserved. He redeemed my soul from going down to the pit, and I will live to enjoy the light.'

"God does all these things to a man—twice, even three times—to turn back his soul from the pit, that the light of life may shine on him." (33:12–30)

Even though Elihu provided more possibilities for Job to explain his circumstance, he still did not hear Job's complaint. Job did not demand that God restore him to his earlier state. Yes, he did long for that, but that was not the substance of his pleas to God. He wanted to talk with God and understand God's purpose. He wanted to know why such things had happened to him.

This seems to me to be a natural response—to want to know why. Yet it really isn't the most important thing. I realize in the midst of the kind of suffering Job endured, it must seem vital. When we see how ordered the universe is, it is logical to assume everything has an explanation. However, in the midst of that order, there are individual differences. There are also mysteries. If everything had a logical explanation, there would be no place for faith. From Job's perspective, and ours, we must exercise *faith* in God at all times, not just when we can't figure things out on our own. That doesn't mean we should not think or reason. But I believe we have to be careful that we don't try to push reason too far and only use faith as a last resort. This is a delicate balance. The most important thing is our relationship with God. We love Him, and so we trust Him (just as I love you and trust you).

Love,
Dick

Who Can Tell Me How to Escape the Pit That Follows Calamity?

Dearest Dick,

As I read your references to chapters 32 and 33, I was fascinated by one of Elihu's comments in particular.

> "Yet if there is an angel on his side as a mediator, one out of a thousand, to tell a man what is right for him, to be gracious to him and say, 'Spare him from going down to the pit; I have found a ransom for him. . . .'" (33:23–24)

I was puzzled by the phrase "one out of a thousand." It struck me even more as I read Job's words which I felt God was directing me to read today. There it was again! It was slightly different in form, but the connection between the two passages was uncanny. The context of the first, "to tell a man what is right for him," and the setting for the second, "a mortal . . . righteous before God," had been brought to my attention by the similarity of the phrase. Was God showing me how He was answering Job's nagging questions?

> "But how can a mortal be righteous before God? Though one wished to dispute with him, he could not answer him *one time out of a thousand*. His wisdom is profound, his power is vast. Who has resisted him and come out unscathed? He moves mountains without their knowing it and overturns them in his anger. He shakes the earth from its place and makes its pillars tremble. He speaks to the sun and it does not shine; he seals off the light of the stars. He alone stretches out the heavens and treads on the waves of the sea. He is the Maker of the Bear and Orion, the Pleiades and the constellations of the south. He performs wonders that cannot be fathomed, miracles that cannot be counted. When he passes me, I cannot see him; when he goes by, I cannot perceive him. If he snatches away, who can stop him? Who can say to him, 'What are you doing?' God does not restrain his anger; even the cohorts of Rahab cowered at his feet.

> "How then can I dispute with him? How can I find words to argue with him? Though I were innocent, I could not answer him; I could only plead with my Judge for mercy. Even if I summoned him and he responded, I do not believe he would give me a hearing. He would crush me with a storm and multiply my wounds for no reason. He would not let me regain my breath but would overwhelm me with

misery. If it is a matter of strength, he is mighty! And if it is a matter of justice, who will summon him? Even if I were innocent, my mouth would condemn me; if I were blameless, it would pronounce me guilty." (9:2b–20)

Job was so close to the truth in this declaration of despair yet so far away. His words reflected so many of the truths God Himself referred to in chapters 38–40, but Job felt condemned by his own words even that early in his experience. He struggled to express what he believed but was overcome by its wrongness.

"He [God] is not a man like me that I might answer him, that we might confront each other in court. If only there were someone to arbitrate between us, to lay his hand upon us both, someone to remove God's rod from me, so that his terror would frighten me no more. Then I would speak up without fear of him, but as it now stands with me, I cannot." (9:32–35)

Job didn't know what he was requesting. So very often I have been kin to Job in more than physical suffering. When I can't think of anything I have done for which God would condemn me, I forget all about my tongue and all the silly lies that are rolling off of it. I don't know they aren't true, but God does. So it was with Job.

Through that arbitrator he begged for, that mediator, that one out of a thousand, Job would begin to understand what was wrong with his plea. Job had been questioning God and demanding answers as if he could order God around. Eventually Job would admit to God.

"You said, 'Listen now, and I will speak; *I* will *question you,* and *you* shall *answer me.'*" (42:4)

Would you mind if we camp on chapters 32 and 33 for a little while? I have so many questions that are bothering me. I need more time to search for answers. First, did Elihu appear arrogant because of who he was or because of the message he was delivering?

So these three men stopped answering Job, because he was righteous in his own eyes. But Elihu son of Barakel the Buzite, of the family of Ram, became very angry with Job for justifying himself rather than God. He was also angry with the three friends, because they had found no way to refute Job, and yet had condemned him. Now Elihu had waited before speaking to Job because they were older than he. But when he saw that the three men had nothing more to say, his anger was aroused. (32:1–5)

His friends thought Job was righteous in his own eyes, but they believed so for all the wrong reasons. They were trying to make him like other men (verse 3). They thought his sin came *before* the calamity. Elihu knew that Job's problem was that in demanding a hearing with God he was trying to be equal with God and tell God what to do (verse 2). That came *after* the calamity. Would God speak through a calamity about a sin that had not even happened yet?

Elihu seems to indicate that he had shown proper respect in waiting for the older men to finish speaking and even hoped that they would voice his argument.

"I am young in years, and you are old; that is why I was fearful, not daring to tell you what I know. I thought, 'Age should speak; advanced years should teach wisdom.' But it is the spirit in a man, the breath of the Almighty, that gives him understanding. It is not only the old who are wise, not only the aged who understand what is right.

"Therefore I say: Listen to me; I too will tell you what I know. I waited while you spoke, I listened to your reasoning; while you were searching for words, I gave you my full attention. But not one of you has proved Job wrong; none of you has answered his arguments. Do not say, 'We have found wisdom; let God refute him, not man.' But Job has not marshaled his words against me, and I will not answer him with your arguments." (32:6b–14)

He seems to say that his whole purpose was to deliver a message to all who would hear.

"I will show partiality to no one, nor will I flatter any man; for if I were skilled in flattery, my Maker would soon take me away." (32:21–22)

I wonder why he approached Job so cautiously and thought that Job might be afraid of him? Why should an older man be intimidated by a younger one?

"But now, Job, listen to my words; pay attention to everything I say. I am about to open my mouth; my words are on the tip of my tongue. My words come from an upright heart; my lips sincerely speak what I know. The Spirit of God has made me; the breath of the Almighty gives me life. Answer me then, if you can; prepare yourself and confront me. I am just like you before God; I too have been taken from clay. *No fear of me should alarm you*, nor should my hand be heavy upon you.

"But you have said in my hearing—I heard the very words— 'I am pure and without sin; I am clean and free from guilt. Yet God has found fault with me; he

considers me his enemy. He fastens my feet in shackles; he keeps close watch on all my paths.'" (33:1–11)

Even though Elihu begged him to prepare an answer, Job didn't say even one word. Job had ranted about the other long speeches.

"I have heard many things like these; miserable comforters are you all! Will your long-winded speeches never end? What ails you that you keep on arguing? I also could speak like you, if you were in my place; I could make fine speeches against you and shake my head at you. But my mouth would encourage you; comfort from my lips would bring you relief." (16:2–5)

But Elihu's speech was three times as long as the arguments of any of the others, and yet Job didn't say a word in reply. Was he just worn out from arguing, or did he at last feel comforted?

I noticed that God never mentioned Elihu in his reprimand to those who had spoken to Job. If he was arrogant and speaking only his own thoughts about God to Job, it seems to me that God would have scolded him as well. If this was a message from God, and Elihu was simply God's messenger, how could he have not appeared arrogant while heralding the approaching speech of Almighty God Himself? I don't know, but I wonder.

I apologize if my questions seem heavy. They are there inside me and are impatient to find hidden or overlooked meanings. Thank you for putting up with me. I trust you with what goes on inside me. And I trust God to reveal all that He has said in His word to us.

I love you so much,
Sue

LETTER 30

Can Confrontation Bring Comfort?

Dear Sue,

Perhaps Elihu was different from Job's other friends. He was younger and more excited about his message than the others. But, like the other three, Elihu was not there to comfort Job, only to confront him.

"I gave you my full attention. But not one of you has proved Job wrong; none of you has answered his arguments." (32:12)

"Answer me then, if you can; prepare yourself and confront me." (33:5)

Job needed friends who would be with him, not against him, and none of these four did that.

However, Elihu does seem different in some ways. While Job's three older friends were quick to answer using reason and logic, Elihu had been listening.

"I waited while you spoke, I listened to your reasoning; while you were searching for words, I gave you my full attention. But not one of you has proved Job wrong; none of you has answered his arguments." (32:11–12)

But the real difference between Elihu and the others was that Elihu said his understanding came from the Spirit.

"But it is the spirit in a man, the breath of the Almighty, that gives him understanding. It is not only the old who are wise, not only the aged who understand what is right." (32:8–9)

"The Spirit of God has made me; the breath of the Almighty gives me life." (33:4)

It is difficult to know whether this is a reference to divine Spirit or the spirit of man. The term "breath of the Almighty" (32:8) would indicate that he believed God gave him wisdom.

Elihu seemed cautious about being presumptuous.

"I will show partiality to no one, nor will I flatter any man; for if I were skilled in flattery, my Maker would soon take me away." (32:21–22)

However, he doesn't appear to be anything other than a mortal like Job.

"I am just like you before God; I too have been taken from clay. No fear of me should alarm you, nor should my hand be heavy upon you." (33:6–7)

Elihu and the others felt that to question God was never appropriate. They thought Job was wrong to raise any question about things he did not understand.

"But I tell you, in this you are not right, for God is greater than man. Why do you complain to him that he answers none of man's words?" (33:12–13)

Are we always wrong to approach God with our questions? Are all questions an expression of doubt? Is it a lack of faith to inquire of God to understand His ways? Wasn't that what Job was doing? He was trying to search within the context of a reverent awe of God.

Perhaps Elihu was arrogant because he felt his message had not yet been delivered by the older men who were reputed to have wisdom. He does seem to have something new to say, such as the section on revelation.

"For God does speak—now one way, now another—though man may not perceive it. In a dream, in a vision of the night, when deep sleep falls on men as they slumber in their beds, he may speak in their ears and terrify them with warnings, to turn man from wrongdoing and keep him from pride, to preserve his soul from the pit, his life from perishing by the sword. Or a man may be chastened on a bed of pain with constant distress in his bones, so that his very being finds food repulsive and his soul loathes the choicest meal. His flesh wastes away to nothing, and his bones, once hidden, now stick out. His soul draws near to the pit, and his life to the messengers of death." (33:14–22)

Look at the concept of a mediator, the "one out of a thousand," which you mentioned earlier. Notice also that he described this mediator as "an angel on his side" and one who would be "gracious to him."

"Yet if there is an angel on his side as a mediator, one out of a thousand, to tell a man what is right for him, to be gracious to him and say, 'Spare him from going down to the pit; I have found a ransom for him'—then his flesh is renewed like a child's; it is restored as in the days of his youth. He prays to God and finds favor with him, he sees God's face and shouts for joy; he is restored by God to his righteous state. Then he comes to men and says, 'I sinned, and perverted what was right, but I did not get what I deserved. He redeemed my soul from going down to the pit, and I will live to enjoy the light.'

"God does all these things to a man—twice, even three times—to turn back his soul from the pit, that the light of life may shine on him." (33:23–30)

Sometimes excitement over one's message can give the appearance of arrogance. However, I'm not sure Job found much "comfort" in Elihu's message. Elihu was just as confrontational as the others had been.

That brings us to the issue of why Job did not answer Elihu. As I looked ahead to the end of Elihu's speeches in chapter 37, I found that the storm (36:33) came after them and the Lord spoke to Job. When the Lord spoke, Job probably forgot about Elihu's message. True, Job didn't interrupt Elihu, but he may not have felt like giving a rebuttal. Whether that was because he was tired of hearing so many arguments or because he didn't feel like Elihu was adding anything new to what he had heard, I don't know.

I can tell you sort of like this fellow Elihu. I'll try not to be jealous! Ha! I'll admit, he said some interesting things, and it is a challenge to understand what he meant.

I love you,
Dick

One Who Is in Pain May Find Comfort
Where Another Would Never Look

Dearest Dick,

I don't think you need to be jealous of Elihu. I agree with you that Elihu was a man just like Bildad and Zophar and Eliphaz and just like you.

Recently a man called you an angel—not because you had sprouted wings or because you were perfect, but because through you he had received a message from God. That did not mean that everything you said was absolutely perfect. That friend of yours could see that you have flaws. But he recognized the "perfect message" God was giving him, and he was thankful that you had pointed him toward that message and enabled him to receive it.

Sometimes I really struggle with understanding life. I want to believe something, and then some exception blocks the way. At times like that you may say just one sentence that you hardly know you utter. God uses that comment to lead me to the light. In that moment you were the "one in a thousand."

At other times you have said to me, "I can hardly wait to preach this new sermon. I really feel that it is a message from God." You preach it in humility, and God allows you to see that He uses it. You preach it again with even a touch of arrogance, and it falls flat.

Angels are not perfect like God. Just look at Satan! Their purpose is not to serve mankind as we are tempted to believe. But among the few things we know that angels did and which were recorded in Scripture were to glorify God and to deliver His message. (They are definitely not pins to wear on our lapels to guard us from misfortune!)

So, as I said before, maybe Elihu's arrogance was because of the message. His words do sound a lot like something we have read before in the arguments of Eliphaz, Zophar, and Bildad, but he always went a little bit further, and that was the part of his message that brought comfort to Job.

For instance, look at Zophar's words. He even accused Job of being unable to learn from experience. He wished God would speak *against* Job.

> "Are all these words to go unanswered? Is this talker to be vindicated? Will your idle talk reduce men to silence? Will no one rebuke you when you mock? You say to God, 'My beliefs are flawless and I am pure in your sight.' Oh, how I wish that God would speak, that he would open his lips against you and disclose to you the secrets of wisdom, for true wisdom has two sides. Know this: God has even forgotten some of your sin.

> "Can you fathom the mysteries of God? Can you probe the limits of the Almighty? They are higher than the heavens—what can you do? They are deeper than the depths of the grave—what can you know? Their measure is longer than the earth and wider than the sea.

> "If he comes along and confines you in prison and convenes a court, who can oppose him? Surely he recognizes deceitful men; and when he sees evil, does he not take note? But a witless man can no more become wise than a wild donkey's colt can be born a man." (11:2–12)

Poor Job! He searched his heart and he just couldn't find the wickedness he was accused of. He mulled over his past looking for sins and wondered if he were deceiving himself. He asked God to weigh him and decide:

> ". . . if I have concealed my sin as men do, by hiding my guilt in my heart because I so feared the crowd and so dreaded the contempt of the clans that I kept silent and would not go outside." (31:33–34)

Now look at Elihu's words. He heard Job and seemed to say: "God is speaking and He is speaking for you."

"But you have said in my hearing—I heard the very words— 'I am pure and without sin; I am clean and free from guilt. Yet God has found fault with me; he considers me his enemy. He fastens my feet in shackles; he keeps close watch on all my paths.'

"But I tell you, in this you are not right, for God is greater than man. Why do you complain to him that he answers none of man's words? For God does speak—now one way, now another—though man may not perceive it." (33:8–14)

"God does all these things to a man—twice, even three times—to turn back his soul from the pit, that the light of life may shine on him." (33:29–30)

You said that it is difficult for you to see how Elihu comforted Job. I have read chapter 10 out loud and felt like the pain reflected in Job's words was pouring from my own heart.

"I loathe my very life; therefore I will give free rein to my complaint and speak out in the bitterness of my soul. I will say to God: Do not condemn me, but tell me what charges you have against me. Does it please you to oppress me, to spurn the work of your hands, while you smile on the schemes of the wicked? Do you have eyes of flesh? Do you see as a mortal sees? Are your days like those of a mortal or your years like those of a man, that you must search out my faults and probe after my sin—though you know that I am not guilty and that no one can rescue me from your hand?

"Your hands shaped me and made me. Will you now turn and destroy me? Remember that you molded me like clay. Will you now turn me to dust again? Did you not pour me out like milk and curdle me like cheese, clothe me with skin and flesh and knit me together with bones and sinews? You gave me life and showed me kindness, and in your providence watched over my spirit.

"But this is what you concealed in your heart, and I know that this was in your mind: If I sinned, you would be watching me and would not let my offense go unpunished. If I am guilty—woe to me! Even if I am innocent, I cannot lift my head, for I am full of shame and drowned in my affliction. If I hold my head high, you stalk me like a lion and again display your awesome power against me. You bring new witnesses against me and increase your anger toward me; your forces come against me wave upon wave.

"Why then did you bring me out of the womb? I wish I had died before any eye saw me. If only I had never come into being, or had been carried straight from the womb to the grave! Are not my few days almost over? Turn away from me so I can have a moment's joy before I go to the place of no return, to the land of gloom and deep shadow, to the land of deepest night, of deep shadow and disorder, where even the light is like darkness." (10:1–22)

Those last verses don't sound like a Christian, for Christians look forward to resurrection from death and eternal life in heaven, not to a place of endless sadness. Yet I identified with his despair. I too have wondered why God had made me and then seemingly deserted me to suffer alone. I too have wondered what secret sin (hidden even from me) had condemned me so. I too have felt weighed down by shame I could not justify.

And from that perspective, I can tell you that I was comforted as I began to read Elihu's (or is it God's?) message in chapter 33. I cannot explain which words soothed my soul. I only know that suddenly the tears stopped and hope began to break on the horizon of my innermost being.

Let's break camp now, my love,
Sue

LETTER 32

Can a Man Serve God for Nothing—
Without "Motivation"?

Darling Sue,

I am glad that God has sometimes spoken to you through me. I would hope that I could always be a vessel that He can use, but I know I am not. God has also used you as an "angel" to speak to me. Many of my sermons are joint ventures, and I am thankful to God for you and your availability to God.

I can see how Elihu's words comfort you. They remind me of teachings from the New Testament.

> "'He redeemed my soul from going down to the pit, and I will live to enjoy the light.'" (33:28)

Another thread that Elihu picked up on in Job's words was:

> "For he says, 'It profits a man nothing when he tries to please God.'" (34:9)

This is similar to Satan's reply to God:

"Does Job fear God for nothing?" (1:9)

Job asked a question like this in 21:15.

"'Who is the Almighty, that we should serve him? What would we gain by praying to him?'"

That brings a very important issue to us, do we serve God for what we can get out of it or do we serve Him just because He is God? I think we would like to say we serve God because we love Him and because His way is right. However, I'm not sure it always washes out that way. When difficulties come we quickly ask, "Why?" as though this shouldn't happen to us because we don't deserve it. So often we hear (and I have preached or taught) that people ought to become Christians in order to be saved. While that is true, our motivation should be on a higher plane. Even simple gratitude is better. But isn't there yet a higher motivation? Shouldn't we serve God for His sake? Not that He needs us, but that He desires that we glorify Him in order that the world may know Him.

I haven't come to a place where Job or any of his friends said this. However, doesn't it go along with your idea about God's concern for Satan? If Job remained faithful to God, even when all was lost, including his health, wouldn't that say there was a man who served God without profit? Even though Job wanted a dialogue with God, he did not curse God as his wife suggested. Job learned much from his experience, and he even repented later, but he never turned away from God. Job believed God and continued to trust Him. He did not request that all that he had before be restored.

While Elihu added some important insight about man's relationship with God, he still believed in the view of God repaying man for what man does wrong.

"So listen to me, you men of understanding. Far be it from God to do evil, from the Almighty to do wrong. He repays a man for what he has done; he brings upon him what his conduct deserves. It is unthinkable that God would do wrong, that the Almighty would pervert justice. Who appointed him over the earth? Who put him in charge of the whole world? If it were his intention and he withdrew his spirit and breath, all mankind would perish together and man would return to the dust.

"If you have understanding, hear this; listen to what I say. Can he who hates justice govern? Will you condemn the just and mighty One?" (34:10–17)

Elihu had an exalted view of God. He believed that God has no need to judge a person because He knows all of man's ways.

> "His eyes are on the ways of men; he sees their every step. There is no dark place, no deep shadow, where evildoers can hide. God has no need to examine men further, that they should come before him for judgment. Without inquiry he shatters the mighty and sets up others in their place. Because he takes note of their deeds, he overthrows them in the night and they are crushed. He punishes them for their wickedness where everyone can see them, because they turned from following him and had no regard for any of his ways. They caused the cry of the poor to come before him, so that he heard the cry of the needy. But if he remains silent, who can condemn him? If he hides his face, who can see him? Yet he is over man and nation alike, to keep a godless man from ruling, from laying snares for the people." (34:21–30)

It is interesting that Elihu called for Job to "be tested to the utmost" as a punishment for his wickedness (34:36). How much more could Job be tested? Did Elihu see what had happened to Job as a test or as punishment? I think he felt that Job was being punished for his sin and would be punished further for rebellion.

> "To his sin he adds rebellion; scornfully he claps his hands among us and multiplies his words against God." (34:37)

I love you,
Dick

When God Doesn't Give an Answer,
GOD IS the Answer

Dearest Dick,

Elihu's words are reassuring even though he was confronting Job. Was he confronting him because he wanted him to be punished for his rebellion or because he wanted him to be saved from his rebellion?

> "Pay attention, Job, and listen to me; be silent, and I will speak. If you have anything to say, answer me; speak up, *for I want you to be cleared.* But if not, then listen to me; be silent, and I will teach you wisdom." (33:31–33)

Sometimes confrontation and helping one to sort out his thoughts are much more comforting than anything that can be said. Misery doesn't necessarily love company! There have been times when you have tried to be comforting by agreeing with me. But I knew I was wrong and didn't know why and longed for someone to set me straight.

In answering your letter I am again perplexed by what I find in Scripture. Once more I find a phrase, which Job had used, repeated by Elihu.

> Then Elihu said: "Hear my words, you wise men; listen to me, you men of learning. For *the ear tests words* as the tongue tastes food. Let us discern for ourselves what is right; let us learn together what is good." (34:1–4)

This is like Job's earlier words.

> "*Does not the ear test words* as the tongue tastes food? Is not wisdom found among the aged? Does not long life bring understanding?" (12:11–12)

Sounds like Jesus' words, "he that hath ears let him hear." Was this a proverb which was merely quoted by both or was Elihu using it in refuting what Job had said about understanding? Compare Job's "Is not wisdom found among the aged?" to Elihu's "Let us discern for ourselves." Elihu seems to be reinforcing Job's beliefs about God which he had arrived at from his own experience.

> "To God belong wisdom and power; counsel and understanding are his. What he tears down cannot be rebuilt; the man he imprisons cannot be released. If he holds back the waters, there is drought; if he lets them loose, they devastate the land. To him belong strength and victory; both deceived and deceiver are his. He leads counselors away stripped and makes fools of judges. He takes off the shackles put on by kings and ties a loincloth around their waist. He leads priests away stripped and overthrows men long established. He silences the lips of trusted advisers and takes away the discernment of elders. He pours contempt on nobles and disarms the mighty. He reveals the deep things of darkness and brings deep shadows into the light. He makes nations great, and destroys them; he enlarges nations, and disperses them. He deprives the leaders of the earth of their reason; he sends them wandering through a trackless waste. They grope in darkness with no light; he makes them stagger like drunkards." (12:13–25)

Elihu seemed to build on Job's statement in order to question Job's challenging God:

"If you have understanding, hear this; listen to what I say. Can he who hates justice govern? Will you condemn the just and mighty One? Is he not the One who says to kings, 'You are worthless,' and to nobles, 'You are wicked,' who shows no partiality to princes and does not favor the rich over the poor, for they are all the work of his hands? They die in an instant, in the middle of the night; the people are shaken and they pass away; the mighty are removed without human hand." (34:16–20)

Also, notice that Elihu had quoted Job to introduce this point about God.

"Job says, 'I am innocent, but God denies me justice. Although I am right, I am considered a liar; although I am guiltless, his arrow inflicts an incurable wound.' What man is like Job, who drinks scorn like water? He keeps company with evil-doers; he associates with wicked men. For he says, 'It profits a man nothing when he tries to please God.'" (34:5–9)

These words reflected Job's thoughts:

"I have become a laughingstock to my friends, though I called upon God and he answered—a mere laughingstock, though righteous and blameless!" (12:4)

This quote may also have come from:

"Yet if I speak, my pain is not relieved; and if I refrain, it does not go away. Surely, O God, you have worn me out; you have devastated my entire household. You have bound me—and it has become a witness; my gauntness rises up and testi-fies against me. God assails me and tears me in his anger and gnashes his teeth at me; my opponent fastens on me his piercing eyes. Men open their mouths to jeer at me; they strike my cheek in scorn and unite together against me. God has turned me over to evil men and thrown me into the clutches of the wicked. All was well with me, but he shattered me; he seized me by the neck and crushed me. He has made me his target; his archers surround me. Without pity, he pierces my kidneys and spills my gall on the ground. Again and again he bursts upon me; he rushes at me like a warrior.

"I have sewed sackcloth over my skin and buried my brow in the dust. My face is red with weeping, deep shadows ring my eyes; yet my hands have been free of violence and my prayer is pure." (16:6–17)

This says to me that Elihu listened carefully to Job's arguments. Elihu called attention to God as the sole source of His sustaining power.

"Who appointed him over the earth? Who put him in charge of the whole world? If it were his intention and he withdrew his spirit and breath, all mankind would perish together and man would return to the dust." (34:13–15)

His intent in this statement seems to be to answer what Job had said in the midst of his terrible despair:

"Turn away from me so I can have a moment's joy. . . ." (10:20b)

What men learn and share with others eventually becomes the wisdom of the ages. We tend to rely on knowledge that has withstood the test of time. After awhile we hardly dare to doubt its truth. But when a person asks new questions or raises exceptions to old answers he is often greeted with vehement arguments such as Job heard.

"Would a wise man answer with empty notions or fill his belly with the hot east wind? Would he argue with useless words, with speeches that have no value? But you even undermine piety and hinder devotion to God. Your sin prompts your mouth; you adopt the tongue of the crafty. Your own mouth condemns you, not mine; your own lips testify against you.

"Are you the first man ever born? Were you brought forth before the hills? Do you listen in on God's council? Do you limit wisdom to yourself? What do you know that we do not know? What insights do you have that we do not have? The gray-haired and the aged are on our side, men even older than your father. Are God's consolations not enough for you, words spoken gently to you? Why has your heart carried you away, and why do your eyes flash, so that you vent your rage against God and pour out such words from your mouth?

"What is man, that he could be pure, or one born of woman, that he could be righteous? If God places no trust in his holy ones, if even the heavens are not pure in his eyes, how much less man, who is vile and corrupt, who drinks up evil like water!" (15:2–16)

No wonder Job said:

"Only a few years will pass before I go on the journey of no return. My spirit is broken, my days are cut short, the grave awaits me. Surely mockers surround me; my eyes must dwell on their hostility.

"Give me, O God, the pledge you demand. Who else will put up security for me? You have closed their minds to understanding; therefore you will not let them triumph. If a man denounces his friends for reward, the eyes of his children will fail.

"God has made me a byword to everyone, a man in whose face people spit. My eyes have grown dim with grief; my whole frame is but a shadow. Upright men are appalled at this; the innocent are aroused against the ungodly." (16:22–17:8)

But his despair could not overcome his hope that God will raise the right- eous.

"Nevertheless, the righteous will hold to their ways, and those with clean hands will grow stronger." (17:9)

There are questions and there are "questions." I believe God gives us inquis- itive minds to learn as much as we can about ourselves and the earth. However, to question God's motives may be beyond our understanding. To do so only builds a barrier between us and God. To see what God does, does not necessitate knowing why He does it. In questioning God, Job was bordering on losing that reverent awe you spoke of. Maybe that's what Elihu meant.

"Suppose a man says to God, 'I am guilty but will offend no more. Teach me what I cannot see; if I have done wrong, I will not do so again.' Should God then reward you on your terms, when you refuse to repent? You must decide, not I; so tell me what you know.

"Men of understanding declare, wise men who hear me say to me, 'Job speaks without knowledge; his words lack insight.'" (34:31–35)

I agree that when God speaks we forget the words of even those who may have pointed us in the right direction. So that could explain Job's lack of response to Elihu.

Maybe your question—is it possible to serve God just because He is God—is the whole point of the book. I think that may be. We are to be like God. If we can accept God as who He says He is, I AM, maybe we can serve Him as He wants us to, simply because we are His. He is our pledge, our ransom, our security that Job and Elihu spoke of. He has paid the price for our freedom from distress. Therefore, we are His servants.

God does what He does because of who He already is. So many of our actions are motivated by what we want to become. Therein lies the temptation to become equal with God. We become bargainers with God. This seems to be the root of our rebellion against Him.

I agree with you that Elihu did not deny that God is just. Man does reap what he sows. But is testing the same thing as punishment? Isn't this whole experience testing Job? I thought we had agreed that Job was not being punished for wrongdoing but was experiencing hardship to the uttermost to prove Satan wrong. *A man will serve God for nothing!* Perhaps Job's testing must continue even longer because he came so close to agreeing with the wicked. Evidently God knew Job's heart and knew that his words came from a state of confusion, not from what Job believed. Very soon after this comment of Elihu, God appeared to Job and his anguish came to an end.

Do you think you could take more than one day on a chapter? My letters just get longer and longer. There are so many issues to talk about.

Love,
Sue

LETTER 34

If We Are Good People, Can We "Get God on Our Side"?

Dear Sue,

Again we have the question, "Will man serve God for nothing?" This time it is the words of Job repeated by Elihu, and it is stated a bit differently.

> "Yet you ask him, 'What profit is it to me, and what do I gain by not sinning?'" (35:3)

In light of Job's circumstances, I guess that would be a pretty logical question. It must have seemed to him that it really didn't matter whether a man sinned or not. On the other hand, there are many practical reasons for not sinning that are beneficial to the persons who choose to refrain from various sins.

However, this wasn't the question Elihu discussed. By his answer he seemed to say that man's sin or sins only affect other people, they don't really affect God. In the same way our righteousness does not give anything to God.

"I would like to reply to you and to your friends with you. Look up at the heavens and see; gaze at the clouds so high above you. If you sin, how does that affect him? If your sins are many, what does that do to him? If you are righteous, what do you give to him, or what does he receive from your hand? Your wickedness affects only a man like yourself, and your righteousness only the sons of men." (35:4–8)

Elihu believed God is not changed by man's actions, so we should not be motivated to "get God on our side." There are no points for being good!

Love,
Dick

LETTER 35

The Body Is Not Supposed to Tell the Mind What It Can and Cannot Do

Dearest Dick,

Those practical benefits for refraining from sin had certainly been enumerated (in a negative way) by Bildad in chapter 18. If this is what happens, surely no one in his right mind would willingly choose to be wicked.

"The lamp of the wicked is snuffed out; the flame of his fire stops burning. The light in his tent becomes dark; the lamp beside him goes out. The vigor of his step is weakened; his own schemes throw him down. His feet thrust him into a net and he wanders into its mesh. A trap seizes him by the heel; a snare holds him fast. A noose is hidden for him on the ground; a trap lies in his path. Terrors startle him on every side and dog his every step. Calamity is hungry for him; disaster is ready for him when he falls. It eats away parts of his skin; death's firstborn devours his limbs. He is torn from the security of his tent and marched off to the king of terrors. Fire resides in his tent; burning sulfur is scattered over his dwelling. His roots dry up below and his branches wither above. The memory of him perishes from the earth; he has no name in the land. He is driven from light into darkness and is banished from the world. He has no offspring or descendants among his people, no survivor where once he lived. Men of the west are appalled at his fate; men of the east are seized with horror. Surely such is the dwelling of an evil man; such is the place of one who knows not God." (18:5–21)

At first Bildad's description of the consequences of sin seemed pretty general, but by the end, he got downright personal. He was judge and jury, and Job was guilty. His comments don't indicate that he had any desire that Job be cleared. Look at his first statement:

"When will you end these speeches? Be sensible, and then we can talk." (18:2)

Is that another way of saying, "Agree with me and then I will listen to you"? Sometimes we have been at odds with each other because you thought one of my off-the-wall comments was directed against you. At such times you have gotten defensive, but, Honey, you never even touch Bildad when it comes to being defensive. He said to Job:

"Why are we regarded as cattle and considered stupid in your sight? You who tear yourself to pieces in your anger, is the earth to be abandoned for your sake? Or must the rocks be moved from their place?" (18:3–4)

Bildad didn't seem to have any idea that this was not a debate to be won by one side or the other. He had no perception of the agony Job was suffering because Job could not find an answer to his dilemma. Bildad believed he understood completely because of what he observed. The problem was much deeper than the physical suffering they could all see. No matter what others said, Job had to keep trying to find the answer that would satisfy his soul.

"How long will you torment me and crush me with words? Ten times now you have reproached me; shamelessly you attack me. If it is true that I have gone astray, my error remains my concern alone. If indeed you would exalt yourselves above me and use my humiliation against me, then know that God has wronged me and drawn his net around me." (19:2–6)

In talking about wickedness, Bildad seemed to point to the smallness of men whereas Elihu tended to point to the greatness of God. This is what Job had not seemed to realize. God is not one to be summoned. He is the One to summon.

I think I had new insight into 35:5–8 this morning when I said to you, "My body just won't cooperate with me." You and I know that is because of the effects of the extreme osteoporosis. In the New Testament, we are called the Body, but Christ is the Head. My body may be far from perfect, but it still tries to do whatever my mind directs it to do. On the other hand, when my body tries to take control and change the way I think about things, that is wrong. If I let my body be in charge, I cease to be who I am. No matter how weak I

may feel or how much it may hurt to stand, I still want to be *me*. That's why it hurts so much when others change the way they relate to me because of my physical condition. I am the same person I was at twenty-five, only a little wiser, I hope.

So it is with us and God. Our brokenness does not diminish His greatness. But just as a pain in my hip can affect the way my foot works, my sin can affect me and it can affect others. However, even though I hurt, the way I think about things is unchanged. I still want to sit in this recliner and pull this computer keyboard into my lap and write. When the pain takes over and won't allow me to sit and work, everything within me cries, "WRONG!" The body is not supposed to tell the mind what it can and cannot do.

Thanks for slowing down.

Love,
Sue

 **LETTER 36**

*Being Still Before God
Is Better Than "Empty Talk"*

Dearest Sue,

I am glad that you have such a great passion about being you. This is significant in your struggle with a not-always-cooperating body. I hope I can always give you the support you need to enforce your desire to be you.

Elihu did have insight into God's nature, and he knew that Job was wrong in trying to summon God. This agrees with the command, "Be still, and know that I am God" (Psalm 46:10a).

In a general statement about the wicked, Elihu seemed to give a direct answer to Job.

> "He [God] does not answer when men cry out because of the arrogance of the wicked. Indeed, God does not listen to their empty plea; the Almighty pays no attention to it. How much less, then, will he listen when you say that you do not see him, that your case is before him and you must wait for him, and further, that

his anger never punishes and he does not take the least notice of wickedness. So Job opens his mouth with empty talk; without knowledge he multiplies words." (35:12–16)

In Job's cry for God to answer him he did seem arrogant. How often we cry out to God like Elihu described.

"Men cry out under a load of oppression; they plead for relief from the arm of the powerful." (35:9)

We run to God in our pain or other tragedy. Again, this seems natural. We cry to God who loves us and we want Him to hear our cry of anguish.

Elihu's description of God is poetic, yet instructive.

"But no one says, 'Where is God my Maker, who gives songs in the night, who teaches more to us than to the beasts of the earth and makes us wiser than the birds of the air?'" (35:10–11)

He saw God as One who is good and gives good things to His people. There is great comfort from His "songs in the night." God's wisdom is greater than any.

I believe Elihu was saying that periods of affliction are times to come to God. We don't have to ask and plead with Him. He knows our plight, and He cares about us. To be still before Him in faith is better than summoning Him with "empty talk."

Love,
Dick

LETTER 37

Justice or Injustice?
It All Depends on the Judge

Dearest Dick,

Justice is an interesting issue. Often when we think someone is guilty of a terrible crime, we say, "I hope he gets what he deserves." Yet if the guilty party is a friend or relative, we may comment on the identical crime, "I hope the judge is lenient." We are indeed strange creatures when it comes to our view of justice.

> Then Elihu said, "Do you think this is just? You say, 'I will be cleared by God.'" (35:1–2)

Job had given a lengthy description of his own view of the injustices done to him in chapter 19. He made it plain that if God would only clear his name, all of these would take care of themselves.

> "His anger burns against me; he counts me among his enemies. His troops advance in force; they build a siege ramp against me and encamp around my tent.

> "He has alienated my brothers from me; my acquaintances are completely estranged from me. My kinsmen have gone away; my friends have forgotten me. My guests and my maidservants count me a stranger; they look upon me as an alien. I summon my servant, but he does not answer, though I beg him with my own mouth. My breath is offensive to my wife; I am loathsome to my own brothers. Even the little boys scorn me; when I appear, they ridicule me. All my intimate friends detest me; those I love have turned against me. I am nothing but skin and bones; I have escaped with only the skin of my teeth.

> "Have pity on me, my friends, have pity, for the hand of God has struck me. Why do you pursue me as God does? Will you never get enough of my flesh?" (19:11–22)

> "If you say, 'How we will hound him, since the root of the trouble lies in him,' you should fear the sword yourselves; for wrath will bring punishment by the sword, and then you will know that there is judgment." (19:28–29)

He warned his friends that when God cleared him, they would be judged by God for being so cruel to him during his suffering. But just like people today, this warning fell on deaf ears. Check out these words of Zophar.

> "My troubled thoughts prompt me to answer because I am greatly disturbed. I hear a rebuke that dishonors me, and my understanding inspires me to reply." (20:2–3)

He jumped to his own defense. I want to say, "Oh, Zophar, don't take it so personally. You've been saying harsher things to Job." He evidently did not even realize how much his tirade about just punishment was hurting Job. But again, his defense was to put down Job by implying that Job was a wicked man who was reaping his just rewards.

"Surely you know how it has been from of old, ever since man was placed on the earth, that the mirth of the wicked is brief, the joy of the godless lasts but a moment. Though his pride reaches to the heavens and his head touches the clouds, he will perish forever, like his own dung; those who have seen him will say, 'Where is he?' Like a dream he flies away, no more to be found, banished like a vision of the night. The eye that saw him will not see him again; his place will look on him no more. His children must make amends to the poor; his own hands must give back his wealth. The youthful vigor that fills his bones will lie with him in the dust.

"Though evil is sweet in his mouth and he hides it under his tongue, though he cannot bear to let it go and keeps it in his mouth, yet his food will turn sour in his stomach; it will become the venom of serpents within him. He will spit out the riches he swallowed; God will make his stomach vomit them up. He will suck the poison of serpents; the fangs of an adder will kill him. He will not enjoy the streams, the rivers flowing with honey and cream. What he toiled for he must give back uneaten; he will not enjoy the profit from his trading. For he has oppressed the poor and left them destitute; he has seized houses he did not build.

"Surely he will have no respite from his craving; he cannot save himself by his treasure. Nothing is left for him to devour; his prosperity will not endure. In the midst of his plenty, distress will overtake him; the full force of misery will come upon him. When he has filled his belly, God will vent his burning anger against him and rain down his blows upon him. Though he flees from an iron weapon, a bronze-tipped arrow pierces him. He pulls it out of his back, the gleaming point out of his liver. Terrors will come over him; total darkness lies in wait for his treasures. A fire unfanned will consume him and devour what is left in his tent. The heavens will expose his guilt; the earth will rise up against him. A flood will carry off his house, rushing waters on the day of God's wrath. Such is the fate God allots the wicked, the heritage appointed for them by God." (20:4–29)

Do I hear a touch of jealousy for all the riches Job had accumulated? This seems a bit like, "You're just getting what you deserve." Again, I am reminded how quickly we judge a rich person guilty. In our country we say that "a person is innocent until proven guilty." Nevertheless, if the accused is wealthy, it is not uncommon to hear "I *know* he's guilty" even before the trial begins. How can we expect to understand God's justice if we can't even understand our own?

Love,
Sue

Are the Afflicted Wicked or Righteous?
Maybe They Are Neither

Dear Sue,

Elihu's understanding of God's justice has some unusual features. He acted as a spokesman or messenger for God, as we said earlier, and he indicated his knowledge had come from "afar." Does that imply he had an inspired message? He also claimed his words were not false.

> "Bear with me a little longer and I will show you that there is more to be said in God's behalf. I get my knowledge from afar; I will ascribe justice to my Maker. Be assured that my words are not false; one perfect in knowledge is with you." (36:2–4)

Again, he implied that his message was from one who had the answer. It's hard to know if Elihu was an "angel" or just an arrogant, presumptuous braggart. The more I read his words, though, I am inclined to agree with you that he was a messenger sent from God. However, I still feel a need to test his words against the larger body of biblical truth as I understand it.

I'm intrigued by his categories of people: the wicked, the afflicted, and the righteous. He said:

> "God is mighty, but does not despise men; he is mighty, and firm in his purpose. He does not keep the wicked alive but gives the afflicted their rights. He does not take his eyes off the righteous; he enthrones them with kings and exalts them forever." (36:5–7)

This is one way he was different from Job's other friends. He created a separate category for Job and those who know affliction. He also proposed that the afflicted have a need to repent. By doing so, they identify with the righteous. By refusing, they become like the wicked.

> "But if men are bound in chains, held fast by cords of affliction, he [God] tells them what they have done—that they have sinned arrogantly. He makes them listen to correction and commands them to repent of their evil. If they obey and serve him, they will spend the rest of their days in prosperity and their years in contentment. But if they do not listen, they will perish by the sword and die without knowledge." (36:8–12)

Elihu described their sin as arrogance and called for them to repent. The result of that repentance would be restoration by God—"they will spend the rest of their days in prosperity" (36:11). I realize this is what happened to Job, but it is a problem for me. It gets back to the main issue, "Will man fear God for nothing?"

While the fairy-tale ending of Job, which I almost suspect was added (no technical proof of this), fits into this idea, it seems to me that life doesn't always work that way. If it does, then man really does serve God for a reward. I believe the story of Job could have ended without Job receiving back all of his prosperity. Couldn't Job have been just as content without all his wealth?

I realize I've jumped ahead, but this chapter brought up an issue that has bothered me about the Book of Job. Perhaps we'll find more of an explanation as we continue.

I love you,
Dick

LETTER 39

All the Answers in the World
May Not Be Enough

Dearest Dick,

There is a strange thread that ties this book together. Notice Elihu's words:

> "But if they do not listen, they will perish by the sword and die without knowledge." (36:12)

Are they not very similar to those spoken by Job to his friends?

> ". . . you should fear the sword yourselves; for wrath will bring punishment by the sword, and then you will know that there is judgment." (19:29)

Unlike Elihu, Job seemed to believe that man *will* have all knowledge eventually. "And then you will know that there is judgment" may also be translated "that you may come to know the Almighty." He was telling his friends that if they did not repent of their actions against him, they would come to know God's judgment in death. That would be "knowledge."

On the other hand, Elihu said, "they will perish by the sword and die without knowledge." Was he implying that if Job did not repent and if he continued to insist that he plead his case before God to learn the reason for all his suffering then he would die and be doomed to ask "why" forever? He had already said:

> "So Job opens his mouth with empty talk; without knowledge he multiplies words." (35:16)

Job really believed what he had been saying was worth hearing. He couldn't understand why God did not listen. If he had done wrong, he wanted to hear it from God Himself. Job seemed obsessed with knowing "why."

> "Listen carefully to my words . . . Bear with me while I speak. . . ." (21:2–3)

> "Yet how often is the lamp of the wicked snuffed out? How often does calamity come upon them, the fate God allots in his anger? How often are they like straw before the wind, like chaff swept away by a gale? It is said, 'God stores up a man's punishment for his sons.' Let him repay the man himself, so that he will know it! Let his own eyes see his destruction; let him drink of the wrath of the Almighty. For what does he care about the family he leaves behind when his allotted months come to an end?" (21:17–21)

Job's obsession, or even his affliction, did not necessarily make him wicked. I don't believe Elihu's categories in chapter 36 are exclusive. True, the righteous are not wicked and the wicked cannot be righteous. But the afflicted might be wicked if they sinned arrogantly and might become righteous by repenting. However, he didn't say freedom from affliction resulted from repentance only, but because of totally obeying and serving God. Elihu showed how God deserves obedience and service.

> "But now, Job, listen to my words; pay attention to everything I say. . . . For God does speak. . . . to turn back his [a man's] soul from the pit, that the light of life may shine on him." (33:1, 14a, 30)

> "Pay attention, Job, and listen to me. . . . It is unthinkable that God would do wrong, that the Almighty would pervert justice." (33:31a; 34:12)

> "If you have understanding, hear this; listen to what I say. . . . Will you condemn the just and mighty One?" (34:16–17)

"God has no need to examine men further, that they should come before him for judgment. . . . But if he remains silent, who can condemn him?" (34:23, 29a)

"Should God then reward you on your terms, when you refuse to repent?" (34:33a)

"He does not answer when men cry out because of the arrogance of the wicked. Indeed, God does not listen to their empty plea; the Almighty pays no attention to it." (35:12–13)

"Bear with me a little longer and I will show you that there is more to be said in God's behalf." (36:2)

"God is mighty, but does not despise men; he is mighty, and firm in his purpose." (36:5)

At last he said of the afflicted:

"But if they do not listen, they will . . . die without knowledge." (36:12)

I believe that Elihu was pleading with Job to give up his quest for knowledge and throw himself on the mercy of the Almighty. Did he promise that *all* would be well if Job repented? Maybe. Maybe not. I don't see any promise that *everything* would be restored. "Prosperity and contentment" in God's Kingdom do not equal "things."

I think of our sons. If we see one of them struggling with a problem that we know is strengthening him, we sometimes step aside. Our instincts say to help him, but our love tells us that we must allow him to stand the test alone. He may wonder why we don't step in and make everything right, but he struggles on. He may wonder if we love him. We may secretly weep as we watch him struggle, wanting to envelope him in our arms and reassure him of our love. Nevertheless, our love is strongest when we resist the urge to interfere and we watch him grow through turmoil. When the test is over and the battle is won, we are free to show our love once again. Is our love a reward for standing the test? No. Did we stop loving until the test was passed? No! It was there all along, but part of loving is allowing the loved one to stand alone and to learn to walk on his own.

Love,
Sue

Weak and in Pain, We Do Things
We Vowed We Would Never Do

Dear Sue,

Whether the promise of prosperity and contentment (36:11) is a result of repentance or obedience, it still appears to be a reward. I realize contentment is a natural result of a person's right relationship with God, but the prosperity mentioned would seem to refer to material gain. I think that was and still is part of people's thinking about serving God.

Elihu considered Job sinful but not godless or wicked. He even felt that God would speak to Job in his suffering.

> "The godless in heart harbor resentment; even when he fetters them, they do not cry for help. They die in their youth, among male prostitutes of the shrines. But those who suffer he delivers in their suffering; he speaks to them in their affliction." (36:13–15)

Job was one of those who suffer, to whom God speaks in their affliction. The words of Elihu were certainly different from the other friends. He pictured God as "wooing" Job.

> "He is wooing you from the jaws of distress to a spacious place free from restriction, to the comfort of your table laden with choice food." (36:16)

This is similar to God's words spoken by Hosea when He said He was going to "allure" Israel into the desert and speak tenderly to her (Hosea 2:14).

Elihu saw God drawing Job to Himself and called for Job to respond in repentance of his arrogance. He seemed to feel that Job was inclined to respond differently and turn to evil. In Job's discussions with his three friends, he seems to have moved in that direction.

> "But now you are laden with the judgment due the wicked; judgment and justice have taken hold of you. Be careful that no one entices you by riches; do not let a large bribe turn you aside. Would your wealth or even all your mighty efforts sustain you so you would not be in distress? Do not long for the night, to drag

people away from their homes. Beware of turning to evil, which you seem to prefer to affliction." (36:17–21)

It would be hard to imagine Job resorting to evil, but all of us have that potential. Job vowed (chapter 31) never to do the things Elihu mentioned, but we are all vulnerable to sin, especially when we are weak and in pain as Job was.

Love,
Dick

LETTER 41

We're Never As Sinless As We Imagine

Dearest Dick,

Like us, Job checked his sin list against things he might have unintentionally done to other people. He probably, in all honesty, came out much better than we do.

Many in our generation pride ourselves on the fact that we have not brought dishonor on our family (we may not have consciously honored them, but that's okay); we have not killed anyone (making them wish they were dead with our harsh words doesn't count); we have not committed adultery (if another's marriage is unhappy anyway, we excuse ourselves for our affairs); we haven't stolen anything (employer's time, taxes, children's allotted attention, spouse's dreams, and loose change don't count); we haven't lied about anyone (though we may not have stood up for them when we heard another lie about them); and we haven't wanted what our neighbor has (we just want something a little better). And let the poor help themselves.

Our attitude toward God falls on the light side of our checklist. We don't adhere to any of the other world religions, but we don't consider our adoration of ourselves as worship. We don't kneel before any idol, but we are happy to be seen wearing our "religious symbols." We don't say those bywords that include God's name, but we tell jokes about Him, and in our prayers we tell Him what we think He ought to do. We remember an hour or two of the first half of the Lord's day, but we really need the rest of it to catch up on our work. "God will understand. He loves us, and He knows that our intentions are good. Only deliberate sinners are 'wicked,'" we tell ourselves.

God was sympathetic to Job from the beginning of this book. He was pleased with Job's offerings and even pointed him out as an example of one who served God for nothing. But Job was not as sinless as he himself imagined. When Job was complaining that his plight outweighed his guilt, he certainly didn't consider himself among the wicked.

> "Look at me and be astonished; clap your hand over your mouth. When I think about this, I am terrified; trembling seizes my body. Why do the wicked live on, growing old and increasing in power?" (21:5–7)

Again, like us, he preferred pointing out the wrongs of those around him to examining his own sins. He even suspected that the evil man was better off than he was. He may have been beginning at this point to wonder if his serving God had been for nothing.

> "I know full well what you are thinking, the schemes by which you would wrong me. You say, 'Where now is the great man's house, the tents where wicked men lived?' Have you never questioned those who travel? Have you paid no regard to their accounts—that the evil man is spared from the day of calamity, that he is delivered from the day of wrath? Who denounces his conduct to his face? Who repays him for what he has done? He is carried to the grave, and watch is kept over his tomb. The soil in the valley is sweet to him; all men follow after him, and a countless throng goes before him.
>
> "So how can you console me with your nonsense? Nothing is left of your answers but falsehood." (21:27–34)

I agree that Elihu did not categorize Job as godless.

> "The godless . . . do not cry for help." (36:13)

No one could say that Job had not cried for help. Elihu had pronounced of these godless ones:

> "They die in their youth, among male prostitutes of the shrines." (36:14)

Was this statement somehow connected to Job's thoughts?

> "The womb forgets them, the worm feasts on them; evil men are no longer remembered but are broken like a tree. They prey on the barren and childless woman, and to the widow show no kindness." (24:20–21)

Wasn't the custom that the service of the male prostitutes in the shrines was to insure fertility? The barren and childless and the widow would certainly be easy prey. I was having trouble feeling that this statement by Job was somehow out of place in its context, that it was not connected to the rest of Job's speech. But Elihu seemed to choose it from among other ideas for a response.

If Elihu's promise of prosperity and contentment is truly a *reward*, what was Job being rewarded for when he received the "fairy-tale ending?"

I love you,
Sue

Does God Give Rewards for Repentance?

Dearest Sue,

The reward Job eventually received, according to Elihu's promise (36:11), was because he obeyed by repenting. However, from God's viewpoint, Job was simply restored to his former state after the time of Satan's testing was over.

Part of Elihu's message, it seems to me, was that God is beyond our understanding, His ways are a mystery to us. Elihu pointed out to Job the greatness of God seen through the clouds, thunder, and lightning.

"How great is God—beyond our understanding! The number of his years is past finding out.

"He draws up the drops of water, which distill as rain to the streams; the clouds pour down their moisture and abundant showers fall on mankind. Who can understand how he spreads out the clouds, how he thunders from his pavilion? See how he scatters his lightning about him, bathing the depths of the sea. This is the way he governs the nations and provides food in abundance. He fills his hands with lightning and commands it to strike its mark. His thunder announces the coming storm; even the cattle make known its approach." (36:26–33)

After he described the greatness of God in making the clouds and the storm, then Elihu interpreted the thunder as God's voice.

"At this my heart pounds and leaps from its place. Listen! Listen to the roar of his voice, to the rumbling that comes from his mouth. He unleashes his lightning beneath the whole heaven and sends it to the ends of the earth. After that comes the sound of his roar; he thunders with his majestic voice. When his voice resounds, he holds nothing back. God's voice thunders in marvelous ways; he does great things beyond our understanding." (37:1–5)

Elihu was awed by the majesty of God as he saw Him in nature. It is interesting that when God answered Job it was out of a storm (38:1).

Love,
Dick

                                                             LETTER 43

Pretending We Understand
God Doesn't Make It So

Dearest Dick,

Two people can say what appears to be the same thing, and yet what they communicate is so different. We have learned that in our relationship with each other. We really have to keep discussing something for quite some time before we can be sure that we agree. Eliphaz's question sounds like Elihu's argument (35:7), but Eliphaz went on to accuse Job of committing sins which Elihu only warned Job to beware of (36:18–21).

"Can a man be of benefit to God?" (22:2a)

"Is it for your piety that he rebukes you and brings charges against you? Is not your wickedness great? Are not your sins endless? You demanded security from your brothers for no reason; you stripped men of their clothing, leaving them naked. You gave no water to the weary and you withheld food from the hungry, though you were a powerful man, owning land—an honored man, living on it. And you sent widows away empty-handed and broke the strength of the fatherless. That is why snares are all around you, why sudden peril terrifies you, why it is so dark you cannot see, and why a flood of water covers you." (22:4–11)

Elihu pointed to the greatness of God and his heart leaped at the thought.

"God is exalted in his power. Who is a teacher like him? Who has prescribed his ways for him, or said to him, 'You have done wrong'? Remember to extol his work, which men have praised in song. All mankind has seen it; men gaze on it from afar. . . . At this my heart pounds and leaps from its place." (36:22–25; 37:1)

Eliphaz, on the other hand, gave the natural response, "Look at me, I understand God. I'm not like the wicked." I too have felt that way.

"Is not God in the heights of heaven? And see how lofty are the highest stars! Yet you say, 'What does God know? Does he judge through such darkness? Thick clouds veil him, so he does not see us as he goes about in the vaulted heavens.' Will you keep to the old path that evil men have trod? They were carried off before their time, their foundations washed away by a flood. They said to God, 'Leave us alone! What can the Almighty do to us?' Yet it was he who filled their houses with good things, *so I stand aloof* from the counsel of the wicked.

"The righteous see their ruin and rejoice; the innocent mock them, saying, 'Surely our foes are destroyed, and fire devours their wealth.'" (22:12–20)

From such a stance, it was easy for Eliphaz to tell Job what he should do *and what God would do* if he did.

"Submit to God and be at peace with him; in this way prosperity will come to you. Accept instruction from his mouth and lay up his words in your heart. If you return to the Almighty, you will be restored: If you remove wickedness far from your tent and assign your nuggets to the dust, your gold of Ophir to the rocks in the ravines, then the Almighty will be your gold, the choicest silver for you. Surely then you will find delight in the Almighty and will lift up your face to God. You will pray to him, and he will hear you, and you will fulfill your vows. What you decide on will be done, and light will shine on your ways. When men are brought low and you say, 'Lift them up!' then he will save the downcast. He will deliver even one who is not innocent, who will be delivered through the cleanness of your hands." (22:21–30)

How clever Satan is! We fall into the trap almost every time. Making ourselves equal with God! Pretending we understand Him who is beyond understanding! I know I have been tempted to do this many times. Is this the sin of arrogance?

Love,
Sue

God Never Loses Control

Dear Sue,

Elihu seemed to make that point with Job. He seemed to think that Job's view of God left something to be desired. Elihu himself had a strong view of God's transcendence which defies understanding.

> "God's voice thunders in marvelous ways; he does great things beyond our understanding. He says to the snow, 'Fall on the earth,' and to the rain shower, 'Be a mighty downpour.' So that all men he has made may know his work, he stops every man from his labor. The animals take cover; they remain in their dens. The tempest comes out from its chamber, the cold from the driving winds. The breath of God produces ice, and the broad waters become frozen. He loads the clouds with moisture; he scatters his lightning through them. At his direction they swirl around over the face of the whole earth to do whatever he commands them. He brings the clouds to punish men, or to water his earth and show his love." (37:5–13)

This young friend of Job believed God controlled men by His acts of nature. I think that was his way of saying God is in complete control, and the lives of people and the natural order are interrelated.

The basis for Elihu's belief that God is incomprehensible seems to be that man is unable to understand how God controls the natural order.

> "Listen to this, Job; stop and consider God's wonders. Do you know how God controls the clouds and makes his lightning flash? Do you know how the clouds hang poised, those wonders of him who is perfect in knowledge? You who swelter in your clothes when the land lies hushed under the south wind, can you join him in spreading out the skies, hard as a mirror of cast bronze?" (37:14–18)

I wonder what Elihu would say to a modern scientist who does understand the ways of the clouds? Does that diminish God's greatness? I think not. Even though people can understand how such things happen, that does not take away from God's greatness; in fact, it may enhance it.

Did you notice Elihu used the phrase "him who is perfect in knowledge" (verse 16) to describe God? He used that earlier when he spoke of himself (36:4b). I'm not sure what that indicates, but Elihu did seem to have a close connection to God, in some ways.

Love,
Dick

⌦ **LETTER 45**

Things Worth Knowing
Still Come from "Afar"

Dearest Dick,

I still think that Elihu was talking about God, not himself, when he said,

> "I get my knowledge *from afar;* I will ascribe justice to *my Maker.* Be assured that my words are not false; *one perfect in knowledge* is with you." (36:3–4)

The words "from afar" indicated to me that these were not his own ideas but had been given to him by another. Speaking of his Maker may have been his attempt to identify that Other who was far away. This would appear to reflect the same theology which we heard from Eliphaz, Bildad, Zophar, and even Job—that God is watching man from afar. The next sentence seems to introduce a new theology, the concept of "Immanuel." This would be in keeping with God's unchanging nature. We learn in Matthew 1:23 that "Immanuel" means "God with us." Perhaps Job and his friends understood Elihu to mean himself. But, in accordance with my theory that Elihu was a messenger from God, I believe these phrases were identifying the source of the message.

Yes, Job's view of God left something to be desired. You might even say that the longer he argued with his friends, the more his view of God was lacking. Elihu warned Job that he was about to go over the edge in his thinking.

> "Be careful that no one entices you. . . . Do not long for the night. . . . Beware of turning to evil, which you seem to prefer to affliction." (36:18a, 20a, 21)

He knew that Job was so desperate for relief that he could be tempted to do almost anything. He was in a spiritually weakened condition. But Elihu also knew that God was still "wooing [Job] from the jaws of distress" (36:16a). God was trying to get Job in a frame of mind so that he would hear Him.

I think I would quibble with you on the point of modern scientists understanding the ways of the clouds. I've lived in Oklahoma too long and seen the meteorologists be wrong in their forecast too many times. I agree that they know a lot about the causes and effects of different elements of weather. But the clouds and the winds have a "personality of their own" that still mystifies even the cleverest weatherman. For instance, exactly where the tornado will touch down or if it will touch down at all, how long the front will stall and the torrential floods will keep rising, etc. If they really understood, we could always escape the wrath of the storm.

Just as the description of mining in that day surprised us with the technology, I think the understanding of weather may have been much greater in those days than we would imagine.

"He draws up the drops of water, which *distill as rain* to the streams." (36:27)

Yet, just as we, they could not control it. They could only understand a little of what was happening. But why the rain fell exactly when it did and where the wind would blow, they ascribed to God and so must we.

I love you,
Sue

LETTER 46

God Sometimes Sends a Messenger to
Prepare the Way for Himself

Darling Sue,

Your point is well taken. My comment was intended as a general statement, that today we can explain why many, not all, natural events happen. I realize there is still a gap in man's comprehension of the weather. However, even if our knowledge becomes more precise, that does not diminish our concept of

God. He does not lose control if man understands how the natural order works. He created it and our minds. Although we will never fully comprehend all of God, I believe knowing more about His creation inspires greater appreciation for Him.

Elihu was impressed with the mystery surrounding God, but he was also amazed at God's power and majesty (37:14–18). In addition, he felt that man, Job in particular, could not approach God because of man's sinfulness.

> "Tell us what we should say to him; we cannot draw up our case because of our darkness. Should he be told that I want to speak? Would any man ask to be swallowed up? Now no one can look at the sun, bright as it is in the skies after the wind has swept them clean." (37:19–21)

The illustration of not being able to look at the sun is very graphic. In the same way, God is too great for man to look upon. I think Elihu rose to even greater heights in his argument when he spoke of God's great justice and righteousness.

> "Out of the north he comes in golden splendor; God comes in awesome majesty. The Almighty is beyond our reach and exalted in power; in his justice and great righteousness, he does not oppress. Therefore, men revere him, for does he not have regard for all the wise in heart?" (37:22–24)

That last phrase can also be translated, "for he does not have regard for any who think they are wise." This is clearer to me.

I agree with you about Elihu being a messenger from God. He seems to have prepared the way for God's direct message. Job must have been humbled as he heard this young man. It was necessary that Job bow before his God rather than stand, ready to argue with Him. As James said, "Humble yourselves before the Lord, and he will lift you up" (James 4:10).

I'm so thankful that God is "beyond our reach" because we can always look up to Him who is far greater than we are. We don't really want God to be like us in our frailties. We need Him to be a source of strength for us. However, I'm also glad that God communicates with us. He does care about us, regardless of the circumstances that surround us. Praise God!

I love you,
Dick

When God Chooses to Reveal Himself,
Humility Happens

Dearest Dick,

Yes, it is impossible for man to look at God and live. Yet we have examples in Scripture of men who "saw" the Lord and lived (Isaiah 6:1–5, Acts 26:13–16). However, we must take notice that these who saw God did not understand God as a result of seeing Him. Rather they saw themselves and were humbled before Him so that they could rightly relate to Him. I think we must do the same. Many times our prayers are that we might see God so that we can be sure He is looking at us. He *is* looking at us and constantly drawing us to Himself in order to deliver us from evil. We have that assurance in the Book of Job (36:15–16) and in other Scriptures as well. This is His unchanging activity. He will neither slumber nor sleep (Psalm 121:4).

To see God, however, does not seem to be a matter of man's volition. God shows Himself when He chooses, not when we desire. Perhaps He shows Himself *more often* to those who desire. But we must admit that the timing is His alone.

You said that Elihu felt that man could not approach God because of man's sinfulness. Then why was Elihu so intent on persuading Job what was wrong with his attempt to approach God? He seemed to pour a lot of energy into helping Job to be prepared to meet God.

Maybe you are right in that we should not and cannot initiate the encounter. God never meets us on our terms, not only because of our sinful nature in general, but also because of our sin of arrogance in thinking that it is even possible in particular. I'm sure this must have something to do with the question, "Will we serve God for nothing?"

God does not have regard for the wise because, in comparison to Him, all people are ignorant fools. Why should He regard even the wisest of us? Yet He loves us and is working on our behalf to deliver us—just as we love our own children and their wives and their children and would drop anything to give our full attention to helping any of them. But you and I know how it hurts when one of ours treats us in a condescending manner. I'm sure we have done that to our own parents as well. Thank God, none of ours does that very often. So we have just a glimmer of how God must feel when any of us treats Him as less than God. He just doesn't want to talk to us when we act like that. But when we see Him as He is, we are humbled by our own inadequacy. Only through the sacrifice of His own Son could even He make it possible for us to speak His name.

I am struck by the fact that Elihu at no point seemed to come out and say, "Job, just be humble, and God will answer your prayer." He led Job toward humility by pointing toward God. But, unlike many speakers today, he recognized that humility is something that *happens to you,* like love. You can't just decide to love someone and it happens. In the same way, you can't be truly humble by pretending to the nth degree. Pride will creep back in.

This is the voice of experience talking. Thanks for loving me even when I'm proud. I don't blame you for not wanting to talk to me sometimes. May those times be fewer and farther between!

Love,
Sue

LETTER 48

Defending One's Position Requires Pride

Dearest Sue,

Pride is also one of the sins I struggle with all the time. It can certainly get in the way of a relationship, as we know. Pride keeps us from a pure relationship with God, and it also destroys intimacy between two people. The cure for pride is, as you said, humility, and the way to humility seems to be by way of the presence of God.

Job did develop pride in himself as he sought to defend his position before God. He was a righteous man and did not deserve the treatment he received. However, life is not always played by rules of justice. Job was not "punished" because of his pride. But in the process of proclaiming his innocence, he took his focus off God and turned inward. In doing this, he sought an explanation from God rather than a deeper relationship with God.

Elihu prepared the way for God's message. He was the lightning that precedes the thunder (36:32–33). It is interesting that God came to Job and spoke out of a storm. Perhaps this is what Elihu alluded to in 37:4–5.

Then the Lord answered Job out of the storm. . . . (38:1a)

Again, God used words similar to Elihu's words in 34:35, when He said:

"Who is this that darkens my counsel with words without knowledge?" (38:2)

The phrase "darkens my counsel" seems to mean that Job was trying to advise God by asking questions of Him. Man, at his most intelligent level, may know many things about this world, but no one is intelligent enough to question God in this way.

It is interesting that Job repeatedly said he wanted to talk with God and question Him about His actions, yet God announced that He would do the questioning and Job could answer the questions.

"Brace yourself like a man; I will question you, and you shall answer me." (38:3)

It is impossible to have pride when we face God in His majesty and wonder. Our minds cannot comprehend His being, and we are brought low before Him. Oh, that we might simply trust Him because of *who He is!*

I love you, darling!
Dick

ᠷᠠᡁᠤᠵᠠᠨ   **LETTER 49**

Pride Is a Seed Just Waiting to Grow
but Not in the Presence of God

Dearest Dick,

The last few days have been really tough for me. I managed over the course of the summer to learn a few things I could do without aggravating the pain in my frail bones. If I limited myself to these activities, I was able to work longer hours than I had for many months. It seemed like I was improving. I was almost afraid to think it was true, but I couldn't resist.

On Thursday the carpenters finished the remodeling job, and it was time to hang the new curtains. I sat back and watched as long as I could, but it was nearly impossible to explain exactly how I wanted them to look. The idea was so strong, I just walked over and reached up to adjust the gathers before I could stop myself. The first upward stretch didn't hurt too much so I did it again. But soon the pain was back with a vengeance. Smack into the wall that remains my prison! The pain hadn't gone away after all. I had just learned to live with my back to it. The pride of getting better had almost taken root.

As you said, Job developed pride throughout the narrative of this book. But, just like in all of us, the seed of pride was always there. Experiences of humility before God kill the pride that has grown within us, but pride waits for the opportunity to grow again. It is a lot like the Johnson grass you keep poisoning behind our back fence. Even if you kill every stalk and every blade, somehow it reappears. The water that makes the flowers and the honey-suckle grow just a few feet away also makes that Johnson grass grow. The more Job talked with his friends, the more his pride seemed to grow. Talking and trying to understand didn't cause the pride. It just gave it opportunity to grow along with the discussion. Of course, being unjustly accused seemed to be the perfect fertilizer for Job's pride.

I think, perhaps, "darkens my counsel" may mean even more than to question. Even today we speak of having knowledge as "being enlightened." Since God's knowledge is perfect, the light of His knowledge is perfect and reaches into even the darkest corner to lend understanding. Man has nothing to add to that knowledge but darkness. God may have been comparing anything Job might have to say to Him to darkness. That is all our thoughts could be in God's presence. We cannot add to His knowledge.

Just as in everything else He does, God was very thorough in His questioning of Job (38:4–39:30). Here are but a few samples.

> "Where were you when I laid the earth's foundation? . . . Who marked off its dimensions? . . . Who stretched a measuring line across it? On what were its footings set? . . .

> "Who shut up the sea behind doors? . . .

> "Have you ever given orders to the morning? . . .

"Have you journeyed to the springs of the sea? . . . Have the gates of death been shown to you? . . .

"What is the way to the abode of light? . . .

"Have you entered the storehouses of the snow? . . . Who cuts a channel for the torrents of rain? . . . From whose womb comes the ice? . . .

"Can you bind the beautiful Pleiades? . . .

"Can you raise your voice to the clouds? . . .

"Who provides food for the raven? . . .

"Do you know when the mountain goats give birth? Do you watch when the doe bears her fawn?

"Can you hold him [the wild ox] to the furrow with a harness?

"Do you give the horse his strength? . . . Do you make him leap like a locust? . . ."

On and on, God's questions go. He seemed to leave no area uncovered. Did Job have an answer? I don't think so! Just as we said about Job's suffering, we couldn't think of anything else that could have happened to him, so every question God asked seemed to be pushed to its limit.

"Where were you when I laid the earth's foundation? Tell me, if you understand." (38:4)

Surely the simplest question a man can be asked is "Where were you?" but even that one stumped Job. That first question must have been a humbling experience for him. But as in his suffering, Job must be questioned to the ultimate. He must brace himself even when he was weakened by sickness and by false accusations from his friends. The test must be "to the utmost" (34:36).

I am amazed that even such a test was not enough to convince Satan. Only one who is a "self deceiver" could have resisted.

Love,
Sue

LETTER 50

*Not Knowing the Answers
Is Where Faith Begins*

Dearest Sue,

God's questions to Job point out to him in a unique way that God is the all powerful Creator of everything. God's questions must have brought Job to a place of great humility. The implication from these questions is that God is the sole Creator and man wasn't even formed when God did His magnificent work.

The language of appearance which God used is beautiful imagery. He added some nice touches to the description, such as:

> ". . . while the morning stars sang together and all the angels shouted for joy?" (38:7)

Another vivid picture is the description of how He marked the boundaries for the seas:

> "Who shut up the sea behind doors when it burst forth from the womb, when I made the clouds its garment and wrapped it in thick darkness, when I fixed limits for it and set its doors and bars in place, when I said, 'This far you may come and no farther; here is where your proud waves halt'?" (38:8–11)

Such descriptions increase my faith in God. Throughout this study, I believe I have come to realize more and more the awesome power of God and how perfect He is. I know I can trust Him in whatever He does. He knows the "big picture," and He loves me. I hope I can be more trusting with God, even when difficult times come.

Love,
Dick

LETTER 51

*Talking to God Can Be a
Tongue-Tying Experience*

Dearest Dick,

I remember as a little girl thinking about how very big the world is. That convinced me that only God could have been its creator. When I read:

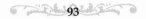

"Who marked off its dimensions? Surely you know! Who stretched a measuring line across it? On what were its footings set, or who laid its cornerstone? . . . " (38:5–6)

I can only answer, "You did, God, only you."

I'm sure Job was keenly aware of this same awesome answer but almost, if not in fact, tongue-tied by his humility. Only after God demanded an answer, he finally stuttered:

"I am unworthy—how can I reply to you? I put my hand over my mouth." (40:4)

Job had been so sure that if God would just grant him an audience, he would have plenty to say. In several passages he had mentioned just what he would ask God (9:33–35; 10:2; 13:3, 20–22; 23:3-4; 31:37). When he at last was in God's presence, he didn't know a thing to say.

This is true of so many situations. Like Job's friend Eliphaz we say, "If it were I, I would. . . . " Yet reality brings us up short. Only by trusting each moment to God, who indeed does see the big picture, can we act appropriately. He understands when we have no words to say, and He leads us through every wilderness.

Love,
Sue

LETTER 52

*God Asks Hard Questions;
We Have No Answers*

Darling Sue,

I find it interesting that in the midst of God's description about the vastness and mystery of the earth, He inserted a brief statement about the wicked and another about death. In asking Job if he had ever been able to order the sunrise or sunset, God identified the wicked with darkness.

"Have you ever given orders to the morning, or shown the dawn its place, that it might take the earth by the edges and shake the wicked out of it? The earth takes shape like clay under a seal; its features stand out like those of a garment. The wicked are denied their light, and their upraised arm is broken." (38:12–15)

Light exposes the wicked and drives them out of the earth. The wicked lose their power in the light. The later symbolism of Jesus as the Light seems to fit into this early analogy. The point for Job may be that he did not understand the ways of God toward the wicked. This is intriguing because elsewhere Job had been called a wicked or at least sinful man.

When God described the vastness of the sea, He described the "gates of death."

> "Have you journeyed to the springs of the sea or walked in the recesses of the deep? Have the gates of death been shown to you? Have you seen the gates of the shadow of death? Have you comprehended the vast expanses of the earth? Tell me, if you know all this." (38:16–18)

Does this indicate that the concept of death or the abode of the dead was thought to be in or under the oceans? This was a mystery to Job and all the people of that day. (Death is still one of the great mysteries.) They had no concept of the resurrection, although Job did raise the question:

> "If a man dies, will he live again?" (14:14a)

You are so right, Job was truly humbled by God through His questions. His righteousness certainly did not put Job on a par with God. Even if Job had lived many more years and been the wisest of sages, he still would not have been able to challenge God.

> "What is the way to the abode of light? And where does darkness reside? Can you take them to their places? Do you know the paths to their dwellings? Surely you know, for you were already born! You have lived so many years!" (38:19–21)

The more we learn about God the more mysteries we find!

Love,
Dick

LETTER 53

"Near Death" Is Not the Real Thing

Dearest Dick,

You are right that death is the eternal mystery. Perhaps because we do not have the testimony of those who have gone there and returned, we remain ignorant. Even those popular writers and speakers who interview on this subject can only speak of *near*-death experiences.

Job spoke of desiring joy before going:

> "to the place of no return, to the land of gloom and deep shadow, to the land of deepest night, of deep shadow and disorder, where even the light is like darkness." (10:21–22)

And in chapter 14, he spoke of a man lying down never to rise again. He wanted to believe that there is a time of renewal, a time when we are no longer held accountable for our sins, but he spoke according to tradition. The sea was a logical place for the gates of death since those who fell into the sea or were lost at sea never returned. It is a shadowy place whose extreme depths do shut out the light.

After all these years when a grandparent or parent dies and a child asks, "Where did they go?" the best we can offer is, "To be with Jesus." If the child presses us for an exact location of that place, we are stumped. We have no more idea than Job did.

Yet God questions him about the recesses of the deep, the gates of death, and the gates of the shadow of death with the same ease He speaks of the nature of snow and hail, lightning and east winds, thunderstorms, and the birth of frost.

> "Have you entered the storehouses of the snow or seen the storehouses of the hail, which I reserve for times of trouble, for days of war and battle? What is the way to the place where the lightning is dispersed, or the place where the east winds are scattered over the earth? Who cuts a channel for the torrents of rain, and a path for the thunderstorm, to water a land where no man lives, a desert with no one in it, to satisfy a desolate wasteland and make it sprout with grass? Does the rain have a father? Who fathers the drops of dew? From whose womb comes the ice? Who gives birth to the frost from the heavens when the waters become hard as stone, when the surface of the deep is frozen?" (38:22–30)

Nothing is beyond God's experience. His questions to Job imply that for all the mysteries that we will never know the answers to, God enjoys an intimate acquaintance with every detail.

Love,
Sue

We Can Run from God or Join Him;
That's Our Choice

Dearest Sue,

When we consider the vastness of the universe with the twinkling constellations, we must acknowledge the greatness and majesty of Creator God. Not only did He create such an intricate yet vast expanse, He also sustains it by His natural laws.

> "Can you bind the beautiful Pleiades? Can you loose the cords of Orion? Can you bring forth the constellations in their seasons or lead out the Bear with its cubs? Do you know the laws of the heavens? Can you set up God's dominion over the earth?" (38:31–33)

Obviously Job, as only a man, was overwhelmed by what God was asking. Surely Job was powerless to "set up God's dominion over the earth." Neither could he call for the thunderstorm.

> "Can you raise your voice to the clouds and cover yourself with a flood of water? Do you send the lightning bolts on their way? Do they report to you, 'Here we are'?" (38:34–35)

God further reminded Job that He alone is the very source of all wisdom and understanding.

> "Who endowed the heart with wisdom or gave understanding to the mind? Who has the wisdom to count the clouds? Who can tip over the water jars of the heavens when the dust becomes hard and the clods of earth stick together?" (38:36–38)

Over and over God reminded Job that he was not in a position to question Him. He did not know enough to even suggest a question to God.

I think this also helped Job to have more faith in God. After all, He is above all, over all, in all, and beyond anything Job could imagine. This could have caused Job to cower before God, afraid of what He might do. However, the other response is to submit to God lovingly, knowing that He knows what is best for us and He has a purpose for our good.

This study has helped me realize anew that God is so faithful. He alone can be trusted. I believe He knows and desires what is best for His Kingdom. My best response is to be in the center of His will, obediently joining Him in what He is doing.

Love,
Dick

The Intimate Story of Creation—
Only God Knows

Dearest Dick,

God's questions to Job almost seem to be an elaboration on the Genesis account of creation. First He talks about giving the earth form.

> "Where were you when I laid the earth's foundation? . . . Who marked off its dimensions? . . . Who stretched a measuring line across it? On what were its footings set, or who laid its cornerstone—while the morning stars sang together and all the angels shouted for joy?" (38:4–7)

Compare this to the first verses of Genesis.

> In the beginning God created the heavens and the earth. Now the earth was formless and empty, darkness was over the surface of the deep, and the Spirit of God was hovering over the waters. (Genesis 1:1–2)

Then He refers to laying boundaries for the seas.

> "Who shut up the sea behind doors when it burst forth from the womb, when I made the clouds its garment and wrapped it in thick darkness, when I fixed limits for it and set its doors and bars in place, when I said, 'This far you may come and no farther; here is where your proud waves halt'?" (38:8–11)

Set this beside the account of creation which is so familiar to us. God's questions in Job almost feel like a peek at the personal touch.

> And God said, "Let the water under the sky be gathered to one place, and let dry ground appear." And it was so. God called the dry ground "land," and the gathered waters he called "seas." And God saw that it was good. (Genesis 1:9–10)

The separation of day and night comes slightly later in Job than in Genesis, but the language is similar.

> "Have you ever given orders to the morning, or shown the dawn its place, that it might take the earth by the edges and shake the wicked out of it? The earth takes shape like clay under a seal; its features stand out like those of a garment. The wicked are denied their light, and their upraised arm is broken." (38:12–15)

> And God said, "Let there be light," and there was light. God saw that the light was good, and he separated the light from the darkness. God called the light "day," and the darkness he called "night." And there was evening, and there was morning—the first day. (Genesis 1:3–5)

God's questions about the vast expanses of the earth and about the dwelling places of light and darkness seem to be tied to His creation of the sky. When He creates the lights in Genesis, He places them in the sky.

> "Have you comprehended the vast expanses of the earth? Tell me, if you know all this.

> "What is the way to the abode of light? And where does darkness reside? Can you take them to their places? Do you know the paths to their dwellings?" (38:18–20)

> And God said, "Let there be an expanse between the waters to separate water from water." So God made the expanse and separated the water under the expanse from the water above it. And it was so. God called the expanse "sky." And there was evening, and there was morning—the second day. (Genesis 1:6–8)

God takes responsibility in His questioning for the creation of vegetation through his bringing forth of precipitation of all kinds. The form of His questions implies that He knows every detail.

> "Who cuts a channel for the torrents of rain, and a path for the thunderstorm, to water a land where no man lives, a desert with no one in it, to satisfy a desolate wasteland and make it sprout with grass?" (38:25–27)

> Then God said, "Let the land produce vegetation: seed-bearing plants and trees on the land that bear fruit with seed in it, according to their various kinds." And it was so. The land produced vegetation: plants bearing seed according to their kinds and trees bearing fruit with seed in it according to their kinds. And God saw that it was good. And there was evening, and there was morning—the third day. (Genesis 1:11–13)

As in Genesis after His reference to vegetation, He points out the stars and their purpose of governing the day and the night. We know this affects plant life.

> "Can you bring forth the constellations in their seasons or lead out the Bear with its cubs? Do you know the laws of the heavens? Can you set up God's dominion over the earth?" (38:32–33)

> And God said, "Let there be lights in the expanse of the sky to separate the day from the night, and let them serve as signs to mark seasons and days and years, and let them be lights in the expanse of the sky to give light on the earth." And it was so. God made two great lights—the greater light to govern the day and the lesser light to govern the night. He also made the stars. God set them in the expanse of the sky to give light on the earth, to govern the day and the night, and to separate light from darkness. And God saw that it was good. And there was evening, and there was morning—the fourth day. (Genesis 1:14–19)

Next in the creation story came the animals. In the same way God had revealed how He made the earth and the sea, the sky, and the first morning to waken the first flower, God turned his questions to the intricacies of the animal kingdom and the secret habits of individual creatures—things that only the Creator would know. It is as if He was pointing out the strength of each animal and explaining the reason for its existence. He gave each one a special purpose.

> "Do you hunt the prey for the lioness and satisfy the hunger of the lions when they crouch in their dens or lie in wait in a thicket? Who provides food for the raven when its young cry out to God and wander about for lack of food?

> "Do you know when the mountain goats give birth? Do you watch when the doe bears her fawn? Do you count the months till they bear? Do you know the time they give birth? They crouch down and bring forth their young; their labor pains are ended. Their young thrive and grow strong in the wilds; they leave and do not return.

> "Who let the wild donkey go free? Who untied his ropes? I gave him the wasteland as his home, the salt flats as his habitat. He laughs at the commotion in the town; he does not hear a driver's shout. He ranges the hills for his pasture and searches for any green thing.

> "Will the wild ox consent to serve you? Will he stay by your manger at night? Can you hold him to the furrow with a harness? Will he till the valleys behind you?

Will you rely on him for his great strength? Will you leave your heavy work to him? Can you trust him to bring in your grain and gather it to your threshing floor?

"The wings of the ostrich flap joyfully, but they cannot compare with the pinions and feathers of the stork. She lays her eggs on the ground and lets them warm in the sand, unmindful that a foot may crush them, that some wild animal may trample them. She treats her young harshly, as if they were not hers; she cares not that her labor was in vain, for God did not endow her with wisdom or give her a share of good sense. Yet when she spreads her feathers to run, she laughs at horse and rider.

"Do you give the horse his strength or clothe his neck with a flowing mane? Do you make him leap like a locust, striking terror with his proud snorting? He paws fiercely, rejoicing in his strength, and charges into the fray. He laughs at fear, afraid of nothing; he does not shy away from the sword. The quiver rattles against his side, along with the flashing spear and lance. In frenzied excitement he eats up the ground; he cannot stand still when the trumpet sounds. At the blast of the trumpet he snorts,'Aha!' He catches the scent of battle from afar, the shout of commanders and the battle cry.

"Does the hawk take flight by your wisdom and spread his wings toward the south? Does the eagle soar at your command and build his nest on high? He dwells on a cliff and stays there at night; a rocky crag is his stronghold. From there he seeks out his food; his eyes detect it from afar. His young ones feast on blood, and where the slain are, there is he." (38:39–39:30)

And God said, "Let the water teem with living creatures, and let birds fly above the earth across the expanse of the sky." So God created the great creatures of the sea and every living and moving thing with which the water teems, according to their kinds, and every winged bird according to its kind. And God saw that it was good. God blessed them and said, "Be fruitful and increase in number and fill the water in the seas, and let the birds increase on the earth." And there was evening, and there was morning—the fifth day.

And God said, "Let the land produce living creatures according to their kinds: livestock, creatures that move along the ground, and wild animals, each according to its kind." And it was so. God made the wild animals according to their kinds, the livestock according to their kinds, and all the creatures that move along the ground according to their kinds. And God saw that it was good. (Genesis 1:20–25)

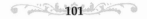

Watching animals teaches us about God and His wisdom. Each has some good point—some purpose (39:16–18). What a useful lesson for us as we ". . . rule over the fish of the sea and the birds of the air, over the livestock, over all the earth, and over all the creatures that move along the ground" (Genesis 1:26).

Love,
Sue

᭙᭙᭙᭙᭙ **LETTER 56**

*Man Is Unworthy to Answer
God's Smallest Question*

Dear Sue,

Surely Job was humbled by God's questions about the "lowly" and "dumb" animals. How little he knew (and we know) about the creatures God so carefully created. Each of the animals (38:39–39:30) has unique characteristics, and God has endowed each with ability that suits its purpose in God's plan.

This should teach us that God has a purpose for us and we should trust Him to accomplish that purpose. God must have been telling Job that He was in charge, He had everything under control.

When God answered Job's prayers by talking with him, Job felt unworthy to speak and had no response.

> The Lord said to Job: "Will the one who contends with the Almighty correct him? Let him who accuses God answer him!"

> Then Job answered the Lord: "I am unworthy—how can I reply to you? I put my hand over my mouth. I spoke once, but I have no answer—twice, but I will say no more." (40:1–5)

Job realized that he was in no position to contend with God or ask Him anything. I think Job began to realize who God is. He came to believe that God is much greater than he had ever thought.

God once again used a storm to speak to Job, just as He did in 38:1, when He began to speak to Job.

"Then the Lord spoke to Job out of the storm." (40:6)

He also used the same method as He did in 38:3.

"Brace yourself like a man; I will question you, and you shall answer me." (40:7)

This was not really the way Job had thought it would be when he asked God to answer him (31:35). Then Job had confidence in his own innocence; now he could only admit that he is without answers to God's questions. I think he took his eyes off himself and put them on God. That will do it for us, won't it? When we realize how utterly matchless God is, we fall before Him in humility.

Love,
Dick

LETTER 57

How Strong Is God?
How Weak Are We?

Dearest Dick,

We should be humble all the time. But so often we reserve humility for those moments when we realize again how great God is. We are so much like Job. We think life treats us unjustly. We would do almost anything to justify ourselves. In our "deepest humility," we often do exactly what Job did—we ask God "why did I deserve this?" It is not easy to have the kind of humility that Job had in 40:4–5. As you mentioned earlier, it is almost impossible to encourage another to serve God without mentioning motivation—what they will get out of it.

God really puts Job to the test. First He gets his attention.

"Would you discredit my justice? Would you condemn me to justify yourself? Do you have an arm like God's, and can your voice thunder like his?" (40:8–9)

Job's words in former chapters when he begs for a hearing with God have implied "yes" to these questions. So God asks Job, if this is true, to prove it by performing a few simple tasks (simple for God).

"*Then* adorn yourself with glory and splendor, and clothe yourself in honor and majesty. Unleash the fury of your wrath, look at every proud man and bring him low, look at every proud man and humble him, crush the wicked where they stand. Bury them all in the dust together; shroud their faces in the grave." (40:10–13)

God's "then" in verse 14 sounds more like "then and only then." He knows that Job cannot do those things He has challenged him to do.

"Then I myself will admit to you that your own right hand can save you." (40:14)

God knows how weak we really are and how strong He really is. We don't seem to know either of those things, but God knows that if we will stop demanding explanations from Him and meditate on the magnificent handiwork of His unspeakable power, we will be reminded and, in humility, find the peace we long for.

Love,
Sue

꿈따뜻 **LETTER 58**

Can God Not Know What He Is Doing?

Darling Sue,

Job did not set out to "discredit [God's] justice" (40:8a). Neither did he intend to "condemn" God in order to justify himself (40:8b). However, he failed to realize when he brought God's justice into question that he was condemning and discrediting Him. Job had said earlier he only wanted to receive an explanation of why bad things had happened to him since he did not accept the explanation of his friends.

When we fail to trust God completely, we, in effect, imply that He does not know what He is doing. I think God wants us to seek understanding of His ways, but we reach a limit on how much we can understand, then we must accept God's actions and know they are just.

God certainly did put Job in his place when He gave him a chance to show his equality with God. Job's voice was no match for the "thunder" (40:9), and

Job did not have "glory and splendor," nor "honor and majesty" (40:10), especially in the afflicted state he was in. If Job had been able to "unleash the fury of [his] wrath" (40:11) against proud people, he would already have consumed his proud "friends." Perhaps God was saying, "See how helpless you have been, even to convince your friends."

All of this, it seems to me, was to show Job that he was not equal with God and he was unable even to contend with God, as Job had said he wanted to do. Job's inability to find God and state his case before Him (23:3–7) was not because Job was so sinful, but because he was not an equal with God. We just don't march into God's presence and demand an audience. We must come humbly before Him, our Lord and our God, ready to receive from His good hand whatever He desires to give us. We know that God loves us and wants the best for us and for His Kingdom. When our desire is to glorify Him and His Kingdom, we identify with God and His purpose.

I know I probably sound simplistic, but the study of Job has strengthened my faith resolve. I just hope I can practice it when the tests come.

I love you,
Dick

LETTER 59

I Can't Always Pray When I Want To

Dearest Dick,

How painful it has been for us when people have implied that if we would just pray, I wouldn't suffer so much. I know that for years you have prayed faithfully for each person in your family every day. Why were these prayers on my behalf not answered? Because of sin? Some Christians would have us believe that. Then, when the pain just continued to get progressively worse, I almost believed them. I began to search my past for what might be responsible for the state I was in.

I found out a lot about my past, but no unconfessed sin that was eating me alive. I was concerned that I entered a period when I did not feel comfortable talking to God. I felt my words had become so empty and I did not understand why. During that time I continued to come before God, but I didn't have anything to say. I just listened. Finally "the day" came when I felt God was urging me to read Job aloud. I wept as I heard myself expressing audibly passages that I myself could have written. I felt that same frustration of just wanting someone to explain what was happening to me.

I had no idea that my telling you about what I had read and your interest in beginning to read Job too and our discussing it that first night would lead to the writing of these letters. I am glad that we chose to take this time to write down our thoughts.

As a young pastor's wife, I felt rebuffed when you occasionally used your seminary learning to refute my ideas. I will admit that some of them were far out. But early in our marriage I learned to be uncomfortable discussing biblical issues with you. I know you have felt uneasy too because you thought that I was challenging your ideas. You have admitted that to me. Lately you seem to feel more ready to hear me. But occasionally I have still felt the "You just don't know . . ." attitude.

In this study of Job, I have not felt that about you. You have been gracious to allow me to go out on my limbs but never threatened to cut me off. I think I have tried to do the same for you. Some of your insights have been very helpful to me. Neither of us is equal to God, although we are human and thus tempted to pretend to be, but both of us are welcomed into His presence in His time when we seek His face in humility.

Your loving wife,
Sue

LETTER 60

If You Can't Control the Creature,
Forget Trying to Control the Creator

Dearest Sue,

This study of Job with you has been a most enjoyable and beneficial journey. It has helped me to be more comfortable with dialogue, and God has taught me so much about who He is and the importance of trust. Your insights have been stimulating and provocative. They have caused me to think more deeply about God's message to me.

In the midst of God's message to Job about Job's lack of strength, God used examples of two exceedingly strong animals to demonstrate that man's strength is very limited. When we think we can stand toe to toe with God, as Job wanted to do, we must realize our place before Him. We need to stop and think how small we are in God's creation. The first of these mighty creatures is called a behemoth, which may refer to an elephant or a hippo.

"Look at the behemoth, which I made along with you and which feeds on grass like an ox. What strength he has in his loins, what power in the muscles of his belly! His tail sways like a cedar; the sinews of his thighs are close-knit. His bones are tubes of bronze, his limbs like rods of iron. He ranks first among the works of God, yet his Maker can approach him with his sword. The hills bring him their produce, and all the wild animals play nearby. Under the lotus plants he lies, hidden among the reeds in the marsh. The lotuses conceal him in their shadow; the poplars by the stream surround him. When the river rages, he is not alarmed; he is secure, though the Jordan should surge against his mouth. Can anyone capture him by the eyes, or trap him and pierce his nose?" (40:15–24)

The key to this description is that this huge animal is one God made, and so He is obviously more powerful than the creature He made. Job should have had no trouble in seeing how helpless he himself was in comparison.

The other creature is called a leviathan. This may refer to a crocodile, or in places it sounds like a mythical sea monster or fire-breathing dragon.

"Can you pull in the leviathan with a fishhook or tie down his tongue with a rope? Can you put a cord through his nose or pierce his jaw with a hook? Will he keep begging you for mercy? Will he speak to you with gentle words? Will he make an agreement with you for you to take him as your slave for life? Can you make a pet of him like a bird or put him on a leash for your girls? Will traders barter for him? Will they divide him up among the merchants? Can you fill his hide with harpoons or his head with fishing spears? If you lay a hand on him, you will remember the struggle and never do it again! Any hope of subduing him is false; the mere sight of him is overpowering. No one is fierce enough to rouse him. Who then is able to stand against me? Who has a claim against me that I must pay? Everything under heaven belongs to me.

"I will not fail to speak of his limbs, his strength and his graceful form. Who can strip off his outer coat? Who would approach him with a bridle? Who dares open the doors of his mouth, ringed about with his fearsome teeth? His back has rows of shields tightly sealed together; each is so close to the next that no air can pass between. They are joined fast to one another; they cling together and cannot be parted. His snorting throws out flashes of light; his eyes are like the rays of dawn. Firebrands stream from his mouth; sparks of fire shoot out. Smoke pours from his nostrils as from a boiling pot over a fire of reeds. His breath sets coals ablaze, and flames dart from his mouth. Strength resides in his neck; dismay goes before him. The folds of his flesh are tightly joined; they are firm and immovable. His chest is hard as rock, hard as a lower millstone. When he rises up, the mighty are terrified; they retreat before his thrashing. The sword that reaches him has no effect, nor does the spear or the dart or the javelin. Iron he treats like straw and bronze like rotten wood. Arrows do not make him flee; slingstones are like chaff to him. A club seems to him but a piece of straw; he laughs at the rattling of the lance. His undersides are jagged potsherds, leaving a trail in the mud like a threshing sledge. He makes the depths churn like a boiling caldron and stirs up the sea like a pot of ointment. Behind him he leaves a glistening wake; one would think the deep had white hair. Nothing on earth is his equal—a creature without fear. He looks down on all that are haughty; he is king over all that are proud." (41:1–34)

The logic of this comparison for Job must be in man's inability and weakness in light of God's power and might. Throughout the description God pointed out Job's or any man's inability to control such a powerful beast. If man can't control a creature which God created, how can a man think he is able to stand before God?

"No one is fierce enough to rouse him. Who then is able to stand against me?" (41:10)

"Fear the Lord," said the writer of Proverbs. It is the beginning of wisdom. Isn't this what Job learned from his experience? Rather than desire to stand in God's presence and question Him, we need to bow before Him, worship Him, and accept. When we do this, we can have complete faith in God to look out for our best interests. He is our enabler, regardless of the circumstances. Thank you, Lord, for caring so much for us!

Love,
Dick

LETTER 61

To Know All There Is to Know about
Wisdom Is Not to Be Wise

Dearest Dick,

I tend to think that the behemoth and the leviathan were much bigger than the elephant or the crocodile. The behemoth had a tail as big as a tree, was taller than poplars, gigantic enough to stand in the middle of a rushing flood and not even notice. The leviathan was covered with shields like a whole army, so protected that not even air could break through. He had a chest like the hardest of rocks and an underside which could leave a trail like the biggest sledge and could stir up an entire sea into thick mud. I think these animals were more like dinosaurs. They were not mythical characters. We know they walked on the earth.

Yes, Job learned that "the fear of the Lord—that is wisdom." But he didn't seem to have that concept at the core of his being until after chapters 38–41. Only then did he reply to the Lord:

> "I know that you can do all things; no plan of yours can be thwarted. You asked, 'Who is this that obscures my counsel without knowledge?' Surely I spoke of things I did not understand, things too wonderful for me to know.
>
> "You said, 'Listen now, and I will speak; I will question you, and you shall answer me.' My ears had heard of you but now my eyes have seen you. Therefore I despise myself and repent in dust and ashes." (42:2–6)

Remember what a beautiful treatise on wisdom we read in chapter 28? How much clearer could one's understanding be? Yet Job said later in chapter 42 that he had only heard these things and tried to live by them. What he said about "the fear of the Lord" in the earlier passage is not untrue. It was good that Job believed these things. They were the foundation on which he lived his life up to the time of this story. But when he had seen the Lord, and not just heard of him, he understood that fear and he repented in dust and ashes. My prayer is that you and I, after sharing this study together with God and seeing Him as never before, will never be the same.

You have referred to the epilogue of the Book of Job as a "fairy-tale ending." I want to look at it with you. Perhaps it isn't as "fairy tale" as we think.

> After the Lord had said these things to Job, he said to Eliphaz the Temanite, "I am angry with you and your two friends, because you have not spoken of me what is right, as my servant Job has. So now take seven bulls and seven rams and go to my servant Job and sacrifice a burnt offering for yourselves. My servant Job will pray for you, and I will accept his prayer and not deal with you according to your folly. You have not spoken of me what is right, as my servant Job has." So Eliphaz the Temanite, Bildad the Shuhite and Zophar the Naamathite did what the Lord told them; and the Lord accepted Job's prayer.
>
> After Job had prayed for his friends, the Lord made him prosperous again and gave him twice as much as he had before. All his brothers and sisters and

everyone who had known him before came and ate with him in his house. They comforted and consoled him over all the trouble the Lord had brought upon him, and each one gave him a piece of silver and a gold ring.

The Lord blessed the latter part of Job's life more than the first. He had fourteen thousand sheep, six thousand camels, a thousand yoke of oxen and a thousand donkeys. And he also had seven sons and three daughters. The first daughter he named Jemimah, the second Keziah and the third Keren-Happuch. Nowhere in all the land were there found women as beautiful as Job's daughters, and their father granted them an inheritance along with their brothers.

After this, Job lived a hundred and forty years; he saw his children and their children to the fourth generation. And so he died, old and full of years. (42:7–17)

First of all, God also chose to speak to Eliphaz whom, according to God's own words, He was angry with. He instructed Eliphaz how to alleviate that anger. Even when He is angry, God is "wooing us from distress." This is also assurance of God's love for those who insist that they know the truth but are dead wrong in their teaching about a God they have never "seen" (42:7–9).

Notice that in God's forgiveness Job was able to forgive these friends who had caused him so much misery by their ignorance. He could *join God* in forgiving them through his prayer for them. That is an idea I hadn't seen before.

After praying for his friends Job again became prosperous. He gave God credit for all his wealth. The person who in chapter 1 was "the greatest man among all the people of the East" still lived in his body, but the defeated Job who sat in ashes had died, and Job was alive again in his new "knowledge of God."

Everyone who had known him before—family and friends—now came to see him. These who couldn't muster the courage to visit while he was so very sick now came to console him because the Lord had been so mean to him. He had had many friends before the calamities struck him down, and a piece of silver and a gold ring from each one surely shortened the road back to prosperity.

But was Job healed? The Scripture does not say so. His sickness obviously withdrew into the background of important things in life, but I see no reference to a new body. Those who visited him comforted and consoled, but there is no reference to rejoicing over healing.

Job again had many possessions, even more than before. He had twice as much, in fact. (They must have had inflation even in those days.)

Again Job had seven sons and three daughters. Just as many as before but never the same as before. New children never replace those we have lost. But Job was able to be happy, and he no longer begged for death to relieve his suffering. He lived to see his new children and their children and even his great-grandchildren and great-great-grandchildren.

We think we have a big family with our five sons and their wives and our growing number of grandchildren! Job had ten children. Let's suppose that each had a spouse, so that makes twenty. Those twenty might have had as many as a hundred children (the second generation) who, in turn, could have married a hundred spouses and had one thousand children (the third generation). In order for the fourth generation to be born, these one thousand great-grandchildren would have married as many as one thousand husbands and wives and might have given birth to another ten thousand great-great-grandchildren. That could easily have been a family of over twelve thousand at his funeral! What a legacy! I'm sure he loved every one of them and rejoiced to the day he died that God had given him this new life of knowing Him.

Love,
Sue

LETTER 62

Are Health and Wealth
Inseparable in "Real Prosperity"?

Darling Sue,

I appreciated reading your insights on the last chapter of Job. Several of those ideas were new to me also. I certainly never realized how much longer he lived and the size of family he must have had, assuming they were all as prolific as he was. That is also an interesting observation about his illness. It might be that when the Book of Job says:

> "After Job had prayed for his friends, the Lord made him prosperous again. . . ."
> (42:10)

That could mean God restored his health as well as his fortune. Prosperity could very well include health, especially in that day and time. It would have been very strange, I think, for Job to have received wealth but not health. That may also explain why all his relatives and friends came to eat with him, to celebrate his "prosperity" (42:11).

"The Lord blessed the latter part of Job's life more than the first." (42:12a)

This could also indicate that God healed him. Don't you think a point would have been made by the writer if Job had been blessed materially but not healed physically?

There are some other interesting things in this final chapter. Job realized that he spoke when he should have been silent (42:3). He recognized the limits of his understanding, and he realized how "wonderful" this knowledge of God was, even though he could not grasp it.

Notice also, he didn't say, "I'm sorry," like we so often do when we sin. He truly repented by despising, or humbling, himself and put dust and ashes on his head as a sign of godly sorrow (42:6). This indicated he understood his place before God. Is this why we often see people kneel to pray? Perhaps this posture would help us remember where we should be in our attitude as we approach God in prayer.

I'm surprised you did not point out to me that Elihu was not included in the list of friends who were told to sacrifice a burnt offering and go to Job so he could pray for them (42:8–9). That further supports your idea that Elihu was not like the others, but he was a heavenly messenger sent by God to prepare the way for God's message.

The final verses contain the "fairy-tale" ending I have referred to earlier (42:12–15). I feel that Job could have found great happiness without the added prosperity because he got his heart right before God. That was the priority matter, not the restoration of his fortune twice over.

But isn't God just like that! He often gives us much more than we deserve if we have proved ourselves good stewards. Also, the other people of that day probably would not have believed Job was in a right relationship with God if he had remained penniless. They still tied health and wealth to divine blessing, and disease and illness to cursing.

Wouldn't that have been a real problem for some of the people if Job had been left with his illness, yet restored to his material prosperity, like you said? While that seems speculative to me, using an argument from silence, it is an interesting theory in light of the current thoughts of the day.

Love,
Dick

*Can We Pray and
Not Ask for Something?*

Dearest Dick,

Just to set the record straight, I don't think I said Elihu was not a man. Why can't he be a man and a messenger from God as well? At least he looked like a man, just like the three "men" who came to Abraham to announce the coming birth of a son (Genesis 18:1–33).

You're right. The other people of that day probably would not have believed Job was in a right relationship with God if he were penniless. It is also true that they *still* tied health and wealth to divine blessing, and disease and illness to cursing. Sounds to me like they would blend right in at a lot of Wednesday night prayer meetings.

And isn't that what Eliphaz and Bildad and Zophar had been saying throughout the entire book? God said, "That's not right." Of course, He may also have been referring to the fact that they may have heard Him speaking to Job in chapters 38 to 41, but they were so set in their beliefs that none of them had seen Him and "had spoken of Him what *was* right" as Job had when he said:

> "I know that you can do all things; no plan of yours can be thwarted. You asked, 'Who is this that obscures my counsel without knowledge?' Surely I spoke of things I did not understand, things too wonderful for me to know.
>
> "You said, 'Listen now, and I will speak; I will question you, and you shall answer me.' My ears had heard of you but now my eyes have seen you. Therefore I despise myself and repent in dust and ashes." (42:2–6)

But what about Satan? Had God stopped loving Satan and wanting him to understand what real faith is? If Job regained everything he had lost, what was to prevent Satan from saying, "See, I told you so. Job waited you out. He knew you'd come through. A man won't fear God for nothing!"

Is God going to give up or is God going to be held hostage by Satan's lie? Or is it a lie? You and I have talked about how hard it is to pray and not ask for *something*. Satan really gets to us, doesn't he?

Love,
Sue

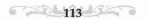 **LETTER 64**

Are Material Blessings Gifts or Rewards?

Dearest Sue,

You bring up interesting points, as always. Another possible explanation for Job's story having such a blessed ending may rest in the fact that there was no concept of heaven among the people of that time. Despite Job's many troubles in life, he received a great reward from God. The story indicates that Job did not serve God in order to receive a reward. If that had been true, Job would have bailed out just like his wife suggested (2:9). However, God's mercy rewarded Job by restoring his wealth and prosperity.

I believe Satan was thwarted by Job's faithfulness to God. While Job questioned God about His actions and wanted to reason with Him, Job never lost faith in God. Such mature faith must have been disgusting to Satan. Job's faith was enhanced by his experience. I think that is what he meant by:

"My ears had heard of you but now my eyes have seen you." (42:5)

I still think the story could have ended with 42:9 and accomplished God's purpose of showing Satan that a man can serve God for nothing. When God then blessed Job with twice as much as he had before, that was evidence of God's grace and mercy. Doesn't that say to us that material blessings may be gifts from God and not rewards?

This doesn't apply to all material prosperity, I realize. Some very wicked people have great material wealth. Just as all sickness is not the result of sin, although some is; neither is all wealth or prosperity the result of God's blessing. The universe just isn't that simple.

Perhaps we can say that God has a purpose for material things in the lives of His people. Job was a good steward of what he received from God. He was generous to those in need, and wealth did not hinder his relationship with God. Job blessed others with his blessings. In Job's poverty and suffering, he learned more about God, and in his prosperity and health, he glorified God with all he had. I hope we can be as faithful with whatever God gives us.

Love,
Dick

Why Did God Make Job Prosperous Again?

Dearest Dick,

Perhaps the book could have ended with 42:9, but the fact is that it didn't. So we must deal with 42:10–17. Was the restoration of Job's wealth and prosperity a reward? If so, then it is a reward *for something*. I wonder if the reward would have been for the good Job had done, for the affliction he had suffered, or for his confession and repentance? This makes way for Job to have acted thus in order to receive the reward, which defeats our argument that Job did indeed "fear God for nothing."

If wealth is a reward, then we must ask why the wicked are also rewarded. Perhaps the answer to this lies in some of Job's earlier observations. He argued that he had seen:

> ". . . that the evil man is spared from the day of calamity. . . ." (21:30a)

> "'He [God] destroys both the blameless and the wicked.'" (9:22b)

So whether in prosperity or in calamity, Job sees no difference between the righteous and the wicked in their life on earth. Prosperity is not a reward. It is God's blessing on all those He loves—the whole world. He agrees with Elihu's words in 36:30–31.

> "See how he scatters his lightning about him, bathing the depths of the sea. This is the way he governs the nations and provides food in abundance."

Therefore, we must understand that Job himself argued against the idea of "reward." So why did the Lord make Job prosperous again? Was it not because this is God's nature—to give good gifts. When Job saw God and repented, he ended his stubborn demands to God and was able to be grateful for *whatever* God bestowed. So God gave good things because that is who He is. Do you agree?

Just why all his family and friends ate with him in his house still baffles me. Job had repented. He had prayed for his three friends. The Lord had made him prosperous again. That's all I see in the record. So why did they come? Was it to comfort and console him? For what, if he was now well? And why did each give him silver and gold?

It seems unlikely to me that Job was still as unsightly as described in 2:7–8, or they would have been unable to eat in his presence. But compare the accounts of these two incidents.

> When Job's three friends . . . heard about all the troubles that had come upon him, they set out . . . to go and sympathize with him and comfort him. (2:11)

> They comforted and consoled him over all the trouble the Lord had brought upon him. . . . (42:11b)

The only difference in these two accounts seems to be that the latter visitors ate with him and gave him gifts. I would like to know if there was a custom that might explain these actions. Of course, not knowing where or when this story occurred complicates that answer, doesn't it?

Why do I always come up with the hard questions? Thanks to you and to God for loving me through them.

Love,
Sue

LETTER 66

*Finding New Meanings May
Require Challenging the Old*

Dearest Sue,

I agree with your discussion and analysis about God restoring Job's fortune. It may have enabled Job once again to have a witness to the people of his day.

The people considered the sick and poor as sinful. Even though Job knew differently, he needed a platform from which to reach the people. Perhaps that is why God restored him. I agree also with you that God likes to give good gifts to His people, but His purpose is more important than such gifts. His gifts to mankind must be a part of His plan and purpose.

When Job's family returned to celebrate with him and give him "a piece of silver and a gold ring" (42:11), it may have been like our visits to people in the hospital. Job's illness may have been slow to heal and surely his restoration took many years. However, perhaps when his family heard that he was "on the mend" they went to rejoice with him. At that time, he was completely destitute and so the gifts would have been appreciated. He may have been able to rebuild his herds, etc., from those gifts. As we know, God often works through people and that may have been God's way for beginning Job's restoration. That may make more sense than God just bringing fourteen thousand sheep, six thousand camels, one thousand yoke of oxen, and one thousand donkeys down the road to Job's house. As the Scripture says, it was during "the latter part of Job's life" he was blessed.

It is unusual, especially in literature of such ancient time, to mention the names of Job's three daughters. None of his earlier children were named in the opening chapter, but in 42:14, all three of the daughters' names are given. This is unusual because we would expect the sons' names to be given rather than those of the daughters. Women did not have high status in Old Testament times and were not considered as important as men. However, Job broke tradition and even gave his daughters an equal part of his inheritance along with their brothers (42:15b).

I thought perhaps there was some special significance in the names so I looked up their meaning. Jemimah means "turtle dove." Keziah means "cassia" or "cinnamon." Keren-Happuch means "painted horn" or "cosmetic box" (*Holman Bible Dictionary*). The meanings of the names are pretty, but I can't find any significance in them. The names seem to denote feminine characteristics, and these were surely appropriate for women who were beautiful:

> "Nowhere in all the land were there found women as beautiful as Job's daughters. . . ." (42:15a)

By the way, while I was looking up names, I found the meaning of the names of three of Job's four friends:

- Eliphaz—"my god is gold"

- Bildad—"the Lord loved"

- Zophar—uncertain

- Elihu—"he is God" (*Holman Bible Dictionary*).

I thought you would enjoy that, especially Elihu's name. That certainly goes with your idea that he was a messenger from God, pointing Job to God.

I have really enjoyed this study with you. I hope we can do more study like this together. You have challenged me to think and look for new meaning, and I hope I have done that for you. At the same time, you have shared some of your innermost feelings with me, and I have appreciated your candor, and I have tried to empathize with your feelings.

I love you,
Dick

LETTER 67

A Road Appears—Beyond the Suffering!

Dearest Dick,

Thank you for looking up the meaning of the names. I do see significance in these beyond the feminine sound. Sometimes names commemorated an event. Haven't you sometimes been so sick you can't taste or smell, and you can hardly hold your eyes open because your fever is so high? Job mentioned how the song had left him (30:31). That happens when you have been sick for a long time.

To me *Jemimah* is saying, "I can hear music again! Beautiful!"

Keziah is saying, "I can smell the earth's intoxicating perfumes as never before. Exhilarating!"

Keren-Happuch is saying, " I can look at beauty once more and feel my heart race!"

Each time Job called one of his little girls to him, he praised God for his restoration—to whatever extent. A very sick person can have *complete* rejoicing for *partial* healing. Just to be "in the land of the living" is enough cause for overflowing joy in one who has been cut off from others by illness.

I will close this study in the same way I started—by reading the entire book of Job aloud. Hopefully we have learned some things about ourselves as well as about God during these past few months. This is what my heart heard in today's reading:

Job's voice rang out in praise and joy, "I have a wonderful family and all the possessions a man could ever want. God has truly blessed me!" (1:1–5).

"Does Job fear God for nothing?" Satan sneered (1:6–12).

Looking about him Job sobbed, "The Lord gave and the Lord has taken away—everything! My possessions! My children!" Then quietly he re-affirmed a lifetime of submission, "May the name of the Lord be praised" (1:13–22).

"Skin for skin! A man will give all he has for his own life." Satan argued (2:1–6).

"The sores cover me from head to foot. The pain afflicts every part of me. Nothing helps. I am tormented day and night," Job observed. Peering deep into the eyes of Eliphaz the Temanite, Bildad the Shuhite, and Zophar the Naamathite, he pled, "Will there be one to help me understand this trouble that would destroy me?" Then, almost in a whisper, "My friends only sit and stare. They have no words of comfort for me. If only I had never been born to experience this suffering" (2:7–3:26).

Thinking he had the answer, Eliphaz offered, "If I were you, I would appeal to God and all would be well. All your possessions would be secure and your children many" (4:1–5:27).

Feeling no sense of comfort Job wailed, "If only my anguish could be weighed. I have no possessions! I have no children! Haven't you noticed? I have even lost the 'self' that I recognized as me. The only thing I have left is my belief that God is. But even He will not speak to me to comfort me. Does He accuse me of wrongdoing as you have done? If only *someone* would tell me *what* I have done wrong. I'm dying!" (6:1–7:21).

"Stop that! Straighten up! Get into a right relationship with God and everything will be just fine. You will have everything you want. You forgot God. That's *your* problem. But repent and all will be well," Bildad reprimanded him (8:1–22).

"How *can* a mortal be righteous before God? He performs wonders that cannot be fathomed, miracles that cannot be numbered. How can I dispute with him?" Job asked. "Even if I were innocent, speaking to Him would be my guilt. He destroys *both* the blameless and the wicked. If only there were someone who *could* speak to God for me. I can find no one. Whether I'm guilty or I'm innocent, I'm drowned in my affliction. Oh, for even a moment of joy before I die" (9:1–10:22).

"How dare you speak of God like that! You deserve *more* punishment," Zophar scolded. "But if you devote your heart to Him and stretch out your hands—all this trouble will be only a fading memory" (11:1–20).

"I'm not a fool," Job cried in defense. "I've always believed what you're saying. Everyone knows it's true. *But* I've always tried to live right and look at me. I'm a laughingstock. Nature itself knows that I'm not responsible for what has happened to me. God is the One who makes one prosper, and then He decides to destroy. I agree. But what is happening to me? I just want God to speak to me—to explain what's going on," he explained. "So be quiet. Your arguments are useless. If only God would summon me, I will answer. Or let me speak and let Him reply. I just want some answers. Man's life is such a fleeting thing, why does God consider it so important? Plants seem to die and then come to life again, but man, when he dies, is dead forever. If only I could die for a little while and not have to suffer God's anger. Then I would like to live again—renewed, where sin is forgotten. But my hope of that is only a dream" (12:1–14:22).

"Who ever heard of such a thing? Living after you're dead! Nonsense! You know that all of us are evil. Why should God care? Be grateful that He is as good as He is. He is not so to the wicked. They are doomed from the word 'go.' Everyone knows it," Eliphaz scoffed (15:1–35).

"I could spout off like you are. But if you were sick, I would try to comfort you. All this talking is not comforting me. God has not only turned against me, He has turned everyone else against me. Oh, there has to be one left who will plead for me to God! My heart cries out for such a one! Soon it will be too late. Only God can provide the ransom necessary to redeem me. Can anyone see any hope for me? Please! Try!" Job pled once more (16:1–17:16).

"Be sensible, Job. You're out of your mind. You're just reaping the rewards of any evil man. So accept it. God is wiping your memory from the face of the earth," Bildad reasoned (18:1–21).

Exasperated, Job asked, "Why do you keep saying I deserved this? Maybe God has turned against me. Must you turn against me too? If only my message could live even though I am dying. I know that my Redeemer lives, and that in the end he will stand upon the earth. And after my skin has been destroyed, yet in my flesh I will see God; I myself will see him with my own eyes—I, and not another. How my heart yearns within me! God put this yearning in me and He will satisfy me" (19:1–29).

Indignant, Zophar angrily replied, "You insult my intelligence! Surely you know that from the beginning of time we have seen that the joy of the wicked does not last. The punishment of bad fortune is the inheritance of the wicked appointed for them by God" (20:1–29).

Searching for a word of hope, quietly Job said once more, "I'm not arguing with you. I'm just trying to make you understand how confused I feel. Look at me! I've tried to do right all my life. I have confessed regularly to God— even for the sins I was not aware of, even for the sins of my children. But all my sons and all my daughters are dead. And look at me!" Confused, he continued, "Yet those we know who are openly wicked say to God, 'Leave us alone! We have no desire to know your ways. Who is the Almighty, that we should serve Him? What would we gain by praying to Him?' and they live on—happy and well. God is not punishing them. I would never agree with them, but God is the One who has blessed them. I wish we could see their punishment but I don't see it.

"I just don't understand why some have such a good life and others live in such misery. It doesn't seem to have anything to do with goodness or wickedness. Those who have seen more than we have will tell you I'm right. Some wicked men never have trouble. Your argument is nonsense!" he concluded (21:1–34).

"Okay, suppose you were blameless," Eliphaz tried again. "What would God gain from that? He is not rebuking you for your goodness! And we can all see that He *is* rebuking you. Think how many sins you have committed when you thought no one would know. Do you think that God cannot see you just because He is busy in heaven?

"Righteous men rejoice when God punishes the wicked. It would be sinful for us to side with you. Come on. Repent and return to prosperity. You trusted in riches. That's your problem. Repent. Then God will do anything you want Him to. He will even deliver a sinful man just because you say to. Claim the power!" he urged (22:1–30).

Job bowed before this latest tirade. "I cannot find Him!" he admitted. "I have followed Him as closely as I know how. I have treasured His words more than anything else in life and tried to do exactly as He commanded. But I've lost touch with Him and I don't know when or why. Is He planning even more horrible experiences for me? I'm terrified! Why won't He let me defend myself?"

As if talking to himself he observed, "Look at all the suffering around us. Why doesn't God set a day for judgement and punish those responsible for all *this* and then let *us* have a fresh start? I just don't understand. Can't God see what is going on? Even we know who the wicked among us are. They are the ones causing suffering. Why must we wait for their death to see their punishment? I just don't understand" (23:1–24:25).

"Only God is perfect. Why should you think you can be righteous enough to stand before God? Even the moon and stars have their flaws. Man is really worthless," Bildad declared (25:1–6).

"Will you never stop?" Job moaned. "I know that no one can comprehend the greatness of God. It is beyond understanding. But you are wrong! I know myself. My conscious is clear. I too would like to see the wicked punished. I too can see God's power. I know that God allots to the wicked a heritage they deserve. Man can do a lot of things. He can light up darkness and find hidden treasures in the earth. He sees where the rivers begin and shows what he has found to others. But where can wisdom be found? Nowhere. It cannot be bought. No price is great enough. Where does wisdom come from? No one knows. Even Death itself does not know. God alone knows. He knows where it dwells and how to get there. Just as He rules the wind and the water, He rules over wisdom. God is the One who said to man, 'The fear of the Lord—that is wisdom, and to shun evil is understanding.'

"How I long for my life like it used to be—when God blessed me, when I could talk to Him and He talked to me. It was a good life in every way one could imagine. But that day is gone. Now I am mocked by the lowliest of mankind. Even the street people detest me. They destroy me. They don't need any help. I have no dignity left. I'm not safe anywhere. I hurt twenty-four hours a day. It chokes me. God, why are you doing this to me? Why don't you answer me? I helped the suffering. I grieved for the poor. But when I hurt, no one helps me. I am so frustrated! The sickness has made me ugly. No one wants to look at me. No one wants to listen to me. They think I'm crazy. The grief is eating me alive!

"When I was young, I pledged that I would not do wrong. I was afraid of the punishment I would receive. I knew God was watching. So my whole life I have been careful to walk the narrow path. If I have strayed from it, I deserve to be punished. But I haven't done wrong. For I dreaded destruction from God, and for fear of his splendor I could not do such things.

"Oh, that I had someone to hear me! If God would just tell me what I have done wrong, I would confess it to the whole world."

With a sigh he resigned, "I don't have anything else to say" (26:1–31:40).

Stepping forward from those who had gathered to watch as these elders tried to help Job, a youth named Elihu began, "I know I'm young. I let the older men finish speaking first. I thought they would speak wisdom. But it is God's spirit in a man that gives him wisdom. Age doesn't matter. I've been listening carefully, and no one has proved Job wrong. Job is not arguing with me just as he was not arguing with you. His argument is with God. I will speak the truth. If I don't, God will take me away."

Gazing at the wretched heap of misery before him, he continued, "Job, listen to me. Does this make sense to you? I heard you say, 'I am pure and without sin. Yet God has found fault with me; He considers me his enemy' and you complain that He will not answer you. God does speak, but you may not have heard. Sometimes He speaks while you're dreaming and sound asleep to warn you against evil. Sometimes when you're sick and think you're dying, He provides a way out. He speaks time after time to redeem you so your soul will not go down into the pit. But you're not hearing Him."

Job lifted his face expectantly. "Listen, Job. Interrupt me if you need to. I want to help you. I want you to have wisdom. Come, let us reason together, all of us. Job has sounded like a wicked man when he says, 'It profits a man nothing when he tries to please God.' Listen, if God merely withdrew, we would all return to dust. Man does reap what his conduct deserves. But that is not punishment from God. Can He who hates justice govern? God rules the earth. He is just. He knows everything. What could He learn from a trial? What could you tell Him that He does not know? But if God remains silent, can you condemn Him? If He hides, can you find Him? If you do wrong and then promise never to do it again, do you deserve a reward? Men, Job doesn't know what he is doing. He doesn't realize what he is saying. He needs help.

"Job, you expect God to clear you. Yet you ask, 'What *profit* is it to me, and *what do I gain* by not sinning?' Look up and think," Elihu urged. "Does your doing right or your doing wrong change God? God chooses not to answer when 'men cry out because of the arrogance of the wicked.' Men don't cry out for the presence of God. They cry out for someone to lift their oppression. God wants you to seek Him—not what He can do for you! Listen, God is trying to speak to you. Can you hear?

"God does not despise men; he is firm in his purpose. He is wooing you from the jaws of distress. Don't turn to God for what you can get out of Him. Don't be convinced that if you will just repent God will give you prosperity. Don't give away your integrity just to save your skin. Remember who God is. He is wiser than anyone, older than anything, greater than everything. Nothing is too big for Him to create. His voice is as loud as the thunder—thunder that shakes everything around us. He rules everything we can see. Everything stops when He comes near. He brings punishment and blessing at the same time. This is how He shows His love. How can we dare speak His Name? "The Almighty is beyond our reach and exalted in power; in His justice and great righteousness, He does not oppress. He looks upon all those who fear him." Elihu finished and sat down to wait with Job (32:1–37:24).

The lightning and thunder that had been threatening all around broke loose in all its fury as the voice of God spoke out of the storm, "Job. Job. Who is this that darkens my counsel with words without knowledge? Job, where were you when I created the world? How did I do it? Who obeyed my commands? Have you ever made anything to compare to my creation? Job, have you ever seen where a man goes when he dies? Or where light comes from? Or darkness? You're an old man, Job. Surely you should know if anyone could.

"Can you tell me where the snow or hail comes from or predict where the lightning will strike? Where does the wind begin? Why does it rain hard and then just sprinkle and then beat down again? Why does it rain on one side of the road and not the other? Who decides when the first frost will come? Can you change the stars or regulate the seasons? Can you give wisdom?

"Can you direct a lion to its prey? Or feed the baby ravens? Where does life come from? Who tends the baby animals of the forest—tiny babes you have never seen? Can you harness the animals I have set free? Can you see the purpose for each of the animals I created? Can you tell a bird where to fly? Answer me" (38:1–40:2).

Speechless before the Almighty Power who interrogated him, Job muttered, "I am unworthy—how can I reply to you? I put my hand over my mouth. I spoke once, but I have no answer—twice, but I will say no more" (40:3–5).

"Brace yourself. Answer me," the Lord commanded. "Am I just? Can you justify yourself and save yourself? Look at the biggest animal that ever walked the earth. I can walk right up to him because I made him. Can you capture him? Look at the biggest creature that ever swam in the ocean. Can you catch him? He is mine! He is fierce beyond imagination—king of the proud. Nothing can touch him. But I can! He is mine!" (40:6–41:34).

Seeing clearly now and feeling comfort course through his veins warming the hardened crust that had become his body, making him pliable as the breath of life washed over him as it had that lump of clay so long ago, Job bowed before God, "I know that you can do all things; no plan of yours can be thwarted. You asked, 'Who is this that obscures my counsel without knowledge?' Surely I spoke of things I did not understand, things too wonderful for me to know."

"You said, 'Listen now, and I will speak; I will question you and you shall answer me.' My ears had heard of you, but now my eyes have seen you. Therefore I despise myself and repent in dust and ashes." At last Job's spirit cried out to the Spirit of God that surrounded him, "I worship you, not for what you can do for me, not for what you give to me, nor for your hedge around me to protect me. I worship you because of WHO YOU ARE" (42:1–17).

This is what I heard as I read the book of Job aloud today. At last God has given *me* the comfort *I* was longing for. No more cause for tears! No more need for explanation! Today I could see—beyond the suffering.

Your loving wife,
Sue

CHARTS

INDEX

CHART 1

COMPARISON OF GOD'S METHODS AND
SATAN'S METHODS CONCERNING JOB

GOD	SATAN
Wooed Job from distress (33:14, 29–30; 36:15–16a; 38:1–3).	Led Sabeans to steal Job's oxen and donkeys and kill his servants (1:14–15).
Allowed Job to practice "fearing the Lord" even before understanding (1:8b; 42:5).	Caused fire to burn Job's sheep and other servants (1:16).
Defined wisdom and gave "the fear of the Lord" (28:28; 40:3–5; 42:1–6).	Led Chaldeans to steal Job's camels and kill more servants (1:17).
	Caused a mighty wind to kill Job's sons and daughters (1:18–19).
	Afflicted Job with painful sores from head to feet (2:7).
Challenged Job's trying to save himself (40:8–14).	Tempted Job's wife to despair (2:9).
Provided one to plead for Job and to tell him the truth (16:18–21; 33:23–24, 31–33).	Deceived friends who tried to comfort Job (4:6,12; 8:5–6; 11:5–6; 15:4–5; 18:12–21; 20:3; 22:21; 25:5–6).
Told the truth because he loved Satan (1:6–8; 2:1–3).	Deceived himself because he hated God (1:9–11; 2:4–5).

CHART 2

COMPARISON OF ADVICE TO JOB

ELIHU

ELIPHAZ, BILDAD, ZOPHAR

DELIVERED MESSAGE FROM GOD

TRUSTED TRADITIONS AND OWN THOUGHTS

"But it is the spirit in a man, the breath of the Almighty, that gives him understanding" (32:8).

"As I have observed . . ." (4:8).

"A word was secretly brought to me . . ." (4:12).

"For I am full of words, and the spirit within me compels me" (32:18).

"I myself have seen . . ." (5:3).

"But if it were I . . ." (5:8).

"I will show partiality to no one, nor will I flatter any man; for if I were skilled in flattery, my Maker would soon take me away" (32:21–22).

"We have examined this . . ." (5:27).

"Ask the former generations . . ." (8:8).

"Yet if you . . . then you will . . ." (11:13–15).

"Listen to me and I will explain . . ." (15:17).

"I hear a rebuke that dishonors me, and my understanding inspires me to reply"(20:3).

"Surely you know how it has been from of old, ever since man was placed on the earth" (20:4).

"Bear with me a little longer and I will show you that there is more to be said in God's behalf. I get my

"If you . . . then the Almighty will . . ." (22:23–25).

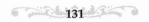

ELIHU (cont.)

ELIPHAZ, BILDAD, ZOPHAR (cont.)

knowledge from afar; I will ascribe justice to my Maker. Be assured that my words are not false; one perfect in knowledge is with you" (36:2–4; *See* 37:16).

"How then can a man be righteous before God? How can one born of woman be pure? If even the moon is not bright and the stars are not pure in his eyes, how much less man, who is but a maggot—a son of man, who is only a worm!" (25:4–6).

WARNED AGAINST SIN

"But now you are laden with the judgment due the wicked; judgment and justice have taken hold of you. Be careful that no one entices you by riches; do not let a large bribe turn you aside" (36:17–18).

ACCUSED JOB OF SIN

"I myself have seen a fool taking root, but suddenly his house was cursed" (5:3).

"Blessed is the man whom God corrects; so do not despise the discipline of the Almighty" (5:17).

"Surely God does not reject a blameless man or strengthen the hands of evildoers" (8:20).

"Do not long for the night, to drag people away from their homes. Beware of turning to evil, which you seem to prefer to affliction" (36:20–21).

"Know this: God has even forgotten some of your sin" (11:6b).

". . . if you put away the sin that is in your hand . . ." (11:14).

"Remember to extol his work . . ." (36:24).

"But you even undermine piety and hinder devotion to God" (15:4).

"Should he be told that I want to speak? Would any man ask to be swallowed up?" (37:20).

"Is not your wickedness great? Are not your sins endless? You demanded security from your brothers for no reason; you stripped men of their clothing, leaving them

ELIHU (cont.)

ELIPHAZ, BILDAD, ZOPHAR (cont.)

naked. You gave no water to the weary and you withheld food from the hungry, though you were a powerful man, owning land—an honored man, living on it. And you sent widows away empty-handed and broke the strength of the fatherless" (22:5–9).

POINTED TO THE GREATNESS OF GOD

POINTED TO OWN UNDERSTANDING

"God is mighty, but does not despise men; he is mighty, and firm in his purpose" (36:5).

"A form stood before my eyes, and I heard a hushed voice" (4:16b).

"Such is the destiny of all who forget God" (8:13a).

"He is wooing you from the jaws of distress . . . " (36:16).

"Oh, how I wish that God would speak, that he would open his lips against you and disclose to you the secrets of wisdom, for true wisdom has two sides"(11:5–6a).

"God is exalted in his power. Who is a teacher like him? Who has prescribed his ways for him, or said to him, 'You have done wrong'? Remember to extol his work, which men have praised in song. All mankind has seen it; men gaze on it from afar. How great is God—beyond our understanding! The number of his years is past finding out" (36:22–26).

"If you return to the Almighty, you will be restored: If you remove wickedness far from your tent and assign your nuggets to the dust, . . . then the Almighty will be your gold, the choicest silver for you. Surely then you will find delight in the Almighty and will lift up your face to God. You will pray to him, and he will hear you, and you will fulfill your vows. What you decide on will be done . . . " (22:23–28).

ELIHU (cont.)

ELIPHAZ, BILDAD, ZOPHAR (cont.)

"At this my heart pounds and leaps from its place. Listen! Listen to the roar of his voice, to the rumbling that comes from his mouth. He unleashes his lightning beneath the whole heaven and sends it to the ends of the earth. After that comes the sound of his roar; he thunders with his majestic voice. When his voice resounds, he holds nothing back. God's voice thunders in marvelous ways; he does great things beyond our understanding" (37:1–5).

"Listen to this, Job; stop and consider God's wonders" (37:14).

"Out of the north he comes in golden splendor; God comes in awesome majesty. The Almighty is beyond our reach and exalted in power; in his justice and great righteousness, he does not oppress" (37:22–23).

POINTED OUT JOB'S ARROGANCE

URGED JOB TO DENY HIS INTEGRITY

"But if men are bound in chains, held fast by cords of affliction, he tells them what they have done— that they have sinned arrogantly" (36:8–9).

"Who has prescribed his ways for him, or said to him, 'You have done wrong'?" (36:23).

"Should he be told that I want to speak?" (37:20a).

"How long will you say such things? Your words are a blustering wind" (8:2).

"Are all these words to go unanswered? Is this talker to be vindicated? Will your idle talk reduce men to silence? Will no one rebuke you when you mock?" (11:2–3).

"Would a wise man answer with empty notions or fill his belly with

ELIHU (cont.)

ELIPHAZ, BILDAD, ZOPHAR (cont.)

the hot east wind? Would he argue with useless words, with speeches that have no value?" (15:2–3).

ADVISED THAT NEITHER WICKEDNESS NOR RIGHTEOUSNESS CHANGE GOD

ADVISED THAT BOTH WICKEDNESS AND RIGHTEOUSNESS CHANGE GOD

"Is he not the One who says to kings, 'You are worthless,' and to nobles, 'You are wicked,' who shows no partiality to princes and does not favor the rich over the poor, for they are all the work of his hands?" (34:18–19).

"But if he remains silent, who can condemn him? If he hides his face, who can see him? Yet he is over man and nation alike" (34:29).

"If you sin, how does that affect him? If your sins are many, what does that do to him? If you are righteous, what do you give to him, or what does he receive from your hand?" (35:6–7).

"This is the way he governs the nations and provides food in abundance" (36:31).

"He brings the clouds to punish men, or to water his earth and show his love" (37:13).

"Will you keep to the old path that evil men have trod? They were carried off before their time, their foundations washed away by a flood. They said to God, 'Leave us alone! What can the Almighty do to us?' Yet it was he who filled their houses with good things, so I stand aloof from the counsel of the wicked" (22:15–18).

"He will deliver even one who is not innocent, who will be delivered through the cleanness of your hands" (22:30).

CHART 3

ELIHU QUOTED JOB AND LED HIM TOWARD GOD

ELIHU	JOB
"But you have said in my hearing—I heard the very words—'I am pure and without sin; I am clean and free from guilt. Yet God has found fault with me; he considers me his enemy'" (33:8–10).	"My face is red with weeping, deep shadows ring my eyes; yet my hands have been free of violence and my prayer is pure" (16:16–17). "Are . . . your years like those of a man, that you must search out my faults and probe after my sin—though you know that I am not guilty and that no one can rescue me from your hand?" (10:5–7).
"'He fastens my feet in shackles; he keeps close watch on all my paths'" (33:11). "But I tell you, in this you are not right, for God is greater than man" (33:12).	"You fasten my feet in shackles; you keep close watch on all my paths" (13:27a).
"Why do you complain to him that he answers none of man's words? For God does speak—now one way, now another—though man may not perceive it" (33:13–14).	"I cry out to you, O God, but you do not answer" (30:20a).
"In a dream, in a vision of the night . . . he may speak in their ears and terrify them with warnings, to turn man from wrongdoing and keep him from pride, to preserve his soul from	"When I think my bed will comfort me and my couch will ease my complaint, even then you frighten me with dreams and terrify me with visions" (7:13–14).

ELIHU (cont.)   **JOB (cont.)**

the pit, his life from perishing by the sword" (33:15–18).

"Yet if there is an angel on his side as a mediator, one out of a thousand, to tell a man what is right . . . and say, '. . . I have found a ransom for him'—then his flesh is renewed. . . . He prays to God . . . he sees God's face . . . he is restored by God . . ." (33:23–26).

"If only there were someone to arbitrate between us, to lay his hand upon us both, someone to remove God's rod from me, so that his terror would frighten me no more" (9:33–34).

"But how can a mortal be righteous before God? Though one wished to dispute with him, he could not answer him one time out of a thousand" (9:2b–3).

"Have I ever said, 'Give something on my behalf, pay a ransom for me . . . deliver me from the hand of the enemy, ransom me . . .'?" (6:22–23).

"Give me, O God, the pledge you demand. Who else will put up security for me?" (17:3).

"For the ear tests words as the tongue tastes food" (34:3).

"Far be it from God to do evil, from the Almighty to do wrong. He repays a man for what he has done; he brings upon him what his conduct deserves. It is unthinkable that God would do wrong, that the Almighty would pervert justice" (34:10b–12).

"Does not the ear test words as the tongue tastes food? Is not wisdom found among the aged? Does not long life bring understanding?" (12:11–12).

"To God belong wisdom and power; counsel and understanding are his. What he tears down cannot be rebuilt; the man he imprisons cannot be released" (12:13–14).

ELIHU (cont.)

"Job says, 'I am innocent, but God denies me justice'" (34:5).

"'Although I am right, I am considered a liar; although I am guiltless, his arrow inflicts an incurable wound'" (34:6).

"For he [Job] says, 'It profits a man nothing when he tries to please God'" (34:9).

"You say, 'I will be cleared by God.' Yet you ask him, 'What profit is it to me, and what do I gain by not sinning?'" (35:2b–3).

JOB (cont.)

"Though I were innocent . . ." (9:15).

"Though I cry, 'I've been wronged!' I get no response; though I call for help, there is no justice" (19:7).

"As surely as God lives, who has denied me justice, the Almighty, who has made me taste bitterness of soul" (27:2).

"The arrows of the Almighty are in me . . ." (6:4).

". . . his archers surround me. Without pity, he pierces my kidneys and spills my gall on the ground" (16:13).

"I have become a laughingstock to my friends, though I called upon God and he answered—a mere laughingstock, though righteous and blameless!" (12:4).

"Have I not wept for those in trouble? Has not my soul grieved for the poor? Yet when I hoped for good, evil came; when I looked for light, then came darkness" (30:25–26).

"Now that I have prepared my case, I know I will be vindicated" (13:18).

"They [the wicked] spend their years in prosperity and go down to the grave in peace. Yet they say to

ELIHU (cont.)	JOB (cont.)
	God, 'Leave us alone! We have no desire to know your ways. Who is the Almighty, that we should serve him? What would we gain by praying to him?'" (21:13–15).
"Men cry out under a load of oppression; they plead for relief from the arm of the powerful" (35:9).	"The groans of the dying rise from the city, and the souls of the wounded cry out for help. But God charges no one with wrongdoing" (24:12).
". . . you say that you do not see him, that your case is before him and you must wait for him, and further, that his anger never punishes and he does not take the least notice of wickedness" (35:14–15).	"When he passes me, I cannot see him" (9:11a).
"He does not keep the wicked alive but gives the afflicted their rights. He does not take his eyes off the righteous; he enthrones them with kings and exalts them forever" (36:6–7).	"Why do the wicked live on, growing old and increasing in power?" (21:7).

CHART 4

COMPARISON OF ELIHU'S MESSAGE
AND GOD'S WORDS/ACTIONS

ELIHU	GOD
"Job speaks without knowledge" (34:35a). "So Job opens his mouth with empty talk; without knowledge he multiplies words" (35:16).	"Who is this that darkens my counsel with words without knowledge? "(38:2).
"Do you think this is just? You say, 'I will be cleared by God.' Yet you ask him, 'What profit is it to me, and what do I gain by not sinning?'" (35:2–3).	"Would you discredit my justice? Would you condemn me to justify yourself?" (40:8).
"Look up at the heavens and see" (35:5a).	"Do you know the laws of the heavens? Can you set up God's dominion over the earth?" (38:33).
"If you sin, how does that affect him? . . . If you are righteous, what do you give to him, or what does he receive from your hand?" (35:6–7).	"Do you have an arm like God's, and can your voice thunder like his?" (40:9).
"But no one says, 'Where is God my Maker, who gives songs in the night, who teaches more to us than to the beasts of the earth and makes us wiser than the birds of the air?'" (35:10–11).	"On what were its footings set, or who laid its cornerstone—while the morning stars sang together and all the angels shouted for joy?" (38:6–7). "Do you hunt the prey for the lioness? . . ." (38:39).

ELIHU (cont.)	GOD (cont.)
	"Do you know when the mountain goats give birth?" (39:1a).
	"Who let the wild donkey go free?" (39:5a).
	"Will the wild ox consent to serve you?" (39:9a).
	". . . for God did not endow her [the ostrich] with wisdom or give her a share of good sense" (39:17).
	"Do you give the horse his strength . . . ?" (39:19).
	"Does the hawk take flight by your wisdom . . . ?" (39:26).
	"Does the eagle soar at your command . . . ?" (39:27).
"But if men are bound in chains, held fast by cords of affliction, he tells them what they have done—that they have sinned arrogantly" (36:8–9).	"Will the one who contends with the Almighty correct him? Let him who accuses God answer him!" (40:2).
"But those who suffer he delivers in their suffering; he speaks to them in their affliction. He is wooing you . . ." (36:15–16).	"Brace yourself like a man; I will question you, and you shall answer me" (38:3).
"Would your wealth or even all your mighty efforts sustain you so you would not be in distress?" (36:19).	"Then adorn yourself. . . . Then I myself will admit to you that your own right hand can save you" (40:10–14).

ELIHU (cont.)   GOD (cont.)

"He draws up the drops of water, which distill as rain to the streams; the clouds pour down their moisture and abundant showers fall on mankind" (36:27–28).

"Does the rain have a father? Who fathers the drops of dew?" (38:28).

"Who can understand how he spreads out the clouds, how he thunders from his pavilion? See how he scatters his lightning about him, bathing the depths of the sea" (36:29–30).

"He fills his hands with lightning and commands it to strike its mark. His thunder announces the coming storm" (36:32–33a).

"Can you raise your voice to the clouds and cover yourself with a flood of water? Do you send the lightning bolts on their way? Do they report to you, 'Here we are'?" (38:34–35).

"He says to the snow, 'Fall on the earth,' and to the rain shower, 'Be a mighty downpour'" (37:6).

"Have you entered the storehouses of the snow or seen the storehouses of the hail . . . ?" (38:22).

"The tempest comes out from its chamber, the cold from the driving winds. The breath of God produces ice, and the broad waters become frozen. He loads the clouds with moisture; he scatters his lightning through them. At his direction they swirl around over the face of the whole earth to do whatever he commands them" (37:9–12).

"Who cuts a channel for the torrents of rain, and a path for the thunderstorm . . . ?" (38:25).

"What is the way to the place where the lightning is dispersed, or the place where the east winds are scattered over the earth?" (38:24).

"From whose womb comes the ice? Who gives birth to the frost from the heavens when the waters become hard as stone, when the surface of the deep is frozen?" (38:29–30).

ELIHU (cont.)	GOD (cont.)
"Do you know how God controls the clouds and makes his lightning flash? Do you know how the clouds hang poised, those wonders of him who is perfect in knowledge?" (37:15–16).	"Who has the wisdom to count the clouds?" (38:37a).
" . . . can you join him in spreading out the skies, hard as a mirror of cast bronze?" (37:18).	"Have you ever given orders to the morning, or shown the dawn its place . . . ?" (38:12).
"Now no one can look at the sun, bright as it is in the skies after the wind has swept them clean" (37:21).	"What is the way to the abode of light? And where does darkness reside? Can you take them to their places? Do you know the paths to their dwellings?" (38:19–20).

INDEX